GENESIS GIRLS
— BOOK TWO —

SARAH LAUGHED

Sarah Laughed
By Paige Henderson
Copyright ©2018

Contact: paige.henderson@fellowshipofthesword.com
All rights reserved.

No portion of this book may be reproduced, stored in a retrieval system, or transmitted in any form or by any means—electronic, mechanical, photocopy, recording, scanning, or other—except for brief quotations in critical reviews or articles, without the prior written permission of the publisher.

Henderson House Publishing

Cover design by Kolton Rogers
Original Artwork (sketch): Surprise by Kendra Ward

The Genesis Girls Series is dedicated to...

My parents, Larry and Rachel, for dedicating me to the Lord and meaning it. Look what that dedication did!

My husband, Richard, for agitating my creativity and propping up my confidence. These Girls have voices because yours is so loud.

My sons, Riley and Maddox (Gus and Buzz), who inspire me to go adventuring. Hey, y'all! Watch this!

My sisters, Leanne and Jennifer, for sharing the backseat of my life—breathing my air, touching my stuff, crossing my lines, and reminding me that, in the end, we are all just real girls.

The "Crack'd Pots" of Vail, Colorado who got me started on this whole Genesis Girl adventure. You know who you are!

Brian and Sabrina who took what I had and squeezed the Life out of it.

Sally who heard the Girls when they were "just" words and listened.

For those who think it's over

TABLE OF CONTENTS

Foreword: Laughter Is Funny That Way	9
When Everything Changed	13
Chasing a Promise	21
Hanging Out In the Harem	31
The Covenant and the Compromise	45
Alone In the Dark	59
The Counterfeit and the Cost	61
The God Who Knows Your Name	73
When God Breathes	87
Why I Laughed	105
Making Peace	129
Our Faithful Promise Maker	139

God has made me laugh.

All who hear will laugh with me.

Genesis 21:6 NLV

FOREWORD
LAUGHTER IS FUNNY THAT WAY

One day I sat for a long time—well, there has been more than one day when I've sat for a long time, but this particular day after sitting for a long time, I got up to move and my leg had fallen asleep. The whole leg. All the way from my hip to my toes was completely numb. If you've ever had an arm or leg fall asleep, you know when you try to move it, you're just dragging dead weight, so when I tried to walk I was more or less lurching as I took a step with my awake leg and then sort of threw my sleeping leg to its next position.

After a few of these "steps" the sensation started coming back to my leg. You know what that feels like, the tingling sensation as the blood starts to flow again? For some reason, that feeling and the realization of how bizarre I must have looked staggering across the room, made me laugh. I'm not talking a little polite snicker. I stopped in the middle of the room and belly-laughed. A moment or two later, my leg was fully awake and I was able to compose myself and move on.

That tingling feeling as a sleeping limb begins to awaken isn't a tickle. It's an altogether odd sensation and on this particular day, it made me laugh but I don't really know why. Laughter is funny that way (pun completely intended). Even though it's the truly universal language, it's difficult to define what it is or why we do it. So difficult that there's an entire science dedicated to the study of laughter. It's called gelotology. That sounds like the study of jellylike desserts to me, but that may be my dessert-centric psyche.

Laughter is laughter for every person from every place in every culture at every time throughout history. I'm not saying the reasons people laugh are all the same, but when you see or hear someone doing it, you automatically know, "Oh, they're laughing." No one has to tell you what those odd noises, face contortions, and body spasms are. And sometimes just seeing or hearing laughter will make you laugh, regardless if you know the laugh-ers or have any idea why they're laughing. You just laugh because they laughed.

The quick answer to why we laugh is we laugh when something is funny, but researchers say most laughter is the result of something other than humor. They don't know what that something is but it's not humor.[1] There are gelotologists (that's a real word) around the world who get up every morning with one goal in mind: Pinpoint how, why, and from where in our magnificently created bodies and brains laughter originates. They've so far come up with some remarkable theories, but the bottom line is, no one knows. Still. Today. No one.

It's no wonder, then, that Sarah's laughter has been misunderstood by so many for so long. Every Sunday school story I heard as a child said Sarah laughed at God when He gave her the greatest news of her by-then very long life. We're told her laugh was sarcastic and derisive and that because God called her out for mocking Him, she lied in an effort to cover up what she'd done. That story never made sense even to my little girl's mind: Why would someone laugh sarcastically at getting the happiest news of her life?

The answer is she didn't. Sarah's story, like so many of the *Genesis Girls*, has been misunderstood, mis-told, or just missed as you're reading your Bible. In case you're not familiar with her, Sarah and her husband, Abraham, birthed (literally) the race of people known throughout history as the Israelites or Hebrews. They are the mother and father of the Jewish people. That means Jesus—yes, Jesus Christ, Jesus Savior of the World, Jesus the Son of God—is one of her direct descendants. She's kind of a big deal, although you will never hear that from her.

I started unwrapping Sarah's story with her laughter, but quickly discovered a woman whose life was marked not by laughter but by disappointment, by feelings of inadequacy, and by fear. I also found a faithful, loving and beloved wife, a woman of dignity, and a woman who longed for—and was given—second chances. In other words, I discovered she was much like me—and you.

As a Daughter of Eve living a skin existence, Sarah's is a story of mistakes, hard lessons, and regret, but as God's 'Princess,' it's also a story of kindness, faithfulness, redemption—and of course, her famous laughter. As you'll see, Sarah's laugh was much more pivotal in the Story of Eternity than even she realized in the moment. I don't want to give anything away, so I will stop before I say too much and turn it over to Sarah so she can tell you why she laughed.

WHEN EVERYTHING CHANGED

Hello. I'm Sarah. If you and I have met before, you may know me as Abraham's wife or maybe Isaac's mother; more than likely as the old woman who laughed at God when He said I'd have a child. Why my spontaneous giggle over such a preposterous idea—a 90-year-old pregnant woman—is so misunderstood and receives such negative attention is a mystery. But it is, and it does.

There's much more to that conversation than one silent albeit significant laugh, although thinking about it now, I admit my heart is laughing again. To grasp the full impact of what happened during that exchange, you need to journey with me to that moment, standing in the doorway of a tent in the desert, and that trip is going to take a few pages to unfold. We will circle back to my laughter farther along the way, but for now, I will tell you two things.

First, I did not laugh "at" God. After so much time and so many mistakes, the words, "I'm coming back about this time next year. When I arrive, your wife Sarah will have a son"[2] were a jolt of pure delight, reviving in me things long dead; more specifically, things I'd killed or let die. Hearing with such certainty that at 90 years old my journey wasn't over, that there was a happy ending still waiting for me somewhere in the desert (and so soon!) my heart erupted with laughter. Of course, my sense of decorum demanded I conceal my mirth from our Guests.

Second, God did not ask me why I laughed because He was angry or His feelings were hurt and He needed an explanation or an apology. The Almighty, who heard the laugh even though it was as silent as a thought, knew why I was laughing. When God asks you a question, He's not looking for information but wants you to experience the fullness of the answer. He wanted me to understand the reason for my laughter, and I want you to understand because when you do, I believe you'll laugh with me.

WONDERING AND WANDERING

That silent laugh was but a moment in a decades-long adventure, so let's move on—for now. My story is of a journey with no known destination, but then, to some extent, that's true for you as well. Regardless of how mundane and predictable life sometimes seems, the truth is that until you arrive, you don't know what's waiting out there under that giant question mark of the future. That my path was through an uncharted wilderness makes my journey somewhat more treacherous but no more unknown than yours.

Had I known setting out that my journey's end was already determined, I'm certain things would have been very different; I would have been very different. I spent a lifetime wondering and wandering. Uncertainty and disappointment were my daily traveling companions. As time went on, I exchanged them for bitterness and (I'm almost embarrassed to admit) unkindness, then for complacency and purposelessness. Until the Day of Laughter.

Not knowing Who it was Abraham and I were following all those years in the desert, most of my energy was spent devising ways to make things happen the way *I* thought they should. That didn't work for me any more than it has for you or anyone else since then. More than once, I detoured from God's path down a side road I believed was a shortcut or more certain way to our final destination. More than once, had it not been for God's sovereignty and unwavering kindness, my journey would have ended in deserved disaster. It took time— lots of time—but I learned.

I was an old woman before I knew I could trust each step of the journey to the One Who'd mapped my trip ahead of time, Who'd created the very wilderness through which we traveled. Trusting Him transforms bitterness to kindness and despair to laughter. By the end of our journey, I hope you trust Him as completely as I learned to and that you know Him as the faithful God, who keeps His covenant and His kindness to a thousand generations.[3]

GETTING TO KNOW ME

My story in the book of *Genesis* in your Bible picks up when I am already 65 years old. Of course, I didn't appear out of the air a woman of that age. Decades and decades of living before my journey began shaped me into the traveler who set off with Abram (that was his name when our journey began) into the desert. I promise no moment-by-moment autobiography, but before we start this trip, we should get to know each other.

I was born and raised in Ur of the Chaldeans in the land of Sumer. On a map, Ur would be approximately in the geographic area you know today as Iraq. Even though it was several thousand years ago, please don't think of me growing up wearing animal skins and playing in the dirt with the family goats. Ur was a major economic hub and the ancient world equivalent of your New York City. I was a city girl.

My friends and our families lived in houses built from baked mud bricks, not in caves. We wore elaborate jewelry crafted by artisans from precious metals and polished stones[4] and dressed in colorful woolen clothing, not animal pelts.[5] As children we didn't play with goats (well, maybe sometimes); we played board games and musical instruments.

There was an education system, a mercantile system, and a banking system. There were markets, libraries, temples, and of course, the Ur Bazaar. Think Galleria.

We may not have had the machines and technology of your world, but we're the culture that gave you the wheel and the 60-second minute. I spent my childhood and youth in Ur visiting the Bazaar, the markets, and the libraries with my mother, her friends, and their children.

Not only was I a city girl, I was a rich city girl. Abram and I grew up in a large, wealthy family. Terah, our father, had several wives and was a successful idol maker. Idol making was a booming business in those days as Sumerian religion included thousands of gods.[6] Yes, thousands. All those gods demanded worship and proper worship required idols. Everyone wanted idols in their homes so they could worship the gods and earn their favor because the favor of the gods was synonymous with wealth.

HAPPY TO MEET ME?

In Sumer generally and Ur particularly, nothing was more important than making money and accumulating possessions.[7] Thousands of gods did not make us more spiritual. It was an indication of the rampant materialism of our culture. The more gods we worshipped, the more favor we could amass, the more money we could make, the happier we believed we'd be. As odd as all that sounds to me now, it was all I knew then.

Something that probably sounds odd to *you* is that Terah was "our father." Abram and I were half-siblings; he was my half-brother. Sumerian custom and culture stipulated marriages be arranged by the patriarch of the family and wedding half-siblings was an effective economic system of protecting all-important family fortunes. The ten-year age gap and having different mothers meant Abram and I spent no time together as children, so I always considered him my husband, not my half-brother—until that distinction became important in our story, as you'll see.

As we grew, my friends and I married husbands selected by our fathers and took our places as the ones visiting the marketplaces with children, sometimes even grandchildren, in tow. Except for me. I'm introduced in your Bible as Sarai (which means "contentious"), Abram's barren wife.[8] Contentious *and* barren. Argumentative *and* unproductive. Mean *and* empty. Happy to meet me? Probably not. After years and years of life as Sarai the Barren, I expected nothing from life but more barrenness. Happily, life seldom turns out as you expect.

Just before I turned 60, Terah moved our family from Ur in southern Sumer to Haran in the north. As the head of the family, when Terah said move, we moved. Moving from Ur actually had been a relief. The more children my friends had, the more I avoided them. I'd grown up with these women, pretending to care for make-believe families in make-believe houses. Their growing families were painful reminders of the emptiness of my grownup house and my grown-old heart.

Gradually, I stopped going to the markets as often. I had servants who could go for me and didn't have to put myself through the humiliation of publicly displaying my childlessness. I know times have changed, but four thousand years ago in Sumer, children weren't only expected, they were required and childlessness was seen as a punishment for having angered one of our gods. A wife's duty—yes, I said duty—was to provide children, particularly male children to perpetuate the family. I knew the judgments of those I passed in the streets, the whispers and condemning looks behind my back. Somehow (unknown to me) I had displeased one of our many gods and my punishment was I could not fulfill my duty as Abram's wife.

More and more I became my name.

THE VOICE

I doubt Terah knew what would happen when we got away from the noise of the city, but it was in Haran that Abram first heard from the One you know as Yahweh or simply God. Eve, who I hope you've had the chance to meet already, knew Him as Elohim, but she walked with Him two thousand years before Abram and I were born.

In Ur we'd heard sketchy stories of a Flood that covered the Earth and whispers of a mysterious God who saved a handful of people from drowning by putting them in a large boat, but those people were not our people (as far as we knew then) and that God certainly wasn't one of our gods. Believe me, if He had been, Terah would have cast an idol for Him. Centuries separated us from the story of The Flood. Anyone who knew the name of that people-saving God was long gone and His name long forgotten. Abram and I knew Him only as The Voice.

Sometimes to hear a nameless, idol-less, destiny-changing Voice, you have to get away from the familiar. Five years after moving us to Haran, Terah died. It was after his death that The Voice spoke to Abram and everything changed. Everything. Not just for me, not just for Abram. Everything. For everybody. Everywhere. Forever. It's at this eternity changing moment our journey begins. It started with the second-most fateful conversation of my life.

CHASING A PROMISE

There are moments that mark a paradigm shift in life. It might be marriage, moving from one place to another, losing a loved one, the birth of a child. These are moments where the trajectory of your path changes forever. For me, that moment was when Abram came home to tell me about The Voice. I remember every detail of that conversation, every thought that passed through my mind.

It was hot, of course, because it was always hot in Haran that time of year, but that day seemed hotter than normal. Just before Abram walked in, I was thinking how hot it was going to be as I baked his favorite barley bread. I was wearing my brown and green wool robe with the dark goat hair belt. I'd bought it at the Bazaar in Ur a few days before we left there. It was soft with wear, but that day it was sticking to my sweaty skin, and I was a little agitated.

I could tell something was on Abram's mind the second I saw him. Once you've been married for as many decades as we had, you know when there's something on your husband's mind. He sat on his favorite cushion and motioned me to join him. I was up to my elbows in barley flour. I gave him a look to say, "A little busy here. Can it wait ten minutes?"

He shook his head. "Sit with me, Sally."

[Sally? All right, something's up. Sally was his pet name for me, but he only used it when he was trying to comfort or cajole me. Oh, Nanna![9] *Did someone die? He'd called me Sally when he told me his brother died. Such a good man, Abram had stepped in and become a second father to our nephew Lot after that. Never having had children of our own, we'd learned to love our nephew as a son.]*

I stopped kneading, went and sat next to him. He took a deep breath and looked me squarely in the eyes.

[Please, Nanna, don't let it be Lot.]

"Sarai, we're moving."

[Moving? Again? Well, at least no one was dead. Moving back to Ur? I'd grown accustomed to Haran's rather small but exotic marketplace and the constant caravans passing through to

the south. Still, I could go back to Ur. We had people there, and there were many more markets and temples. If Abram was going on in the family business, it was a good financial move. Oh, and the Ur Bazaar was the best! Yes, let's move back to Ur. The servants and I can have this place packed up in no time.]

"Going back to Ur! How exciting!" the clapping of my barley flour covered hands left a little dust exclamation point hanging in the air.

"Not Ur." He was looking at me with an intensity that made me a little uncomfortable.

"Not Ur?" my hands and their exclamation point fell into my lap.

"No."

"Okay. Where?" [Where else was there? Surely not one of the settlements we'd passed on our way to Haran.]

"West."

"West. Is that a town I've not heard of or just a direction?"

"A direction."

"And what's west?"

"I'm not sure."

"How far west?" [Hmm. Outside the Haran city wall? Okay. Just because I'd been a city girl all my life didn't mean I couldn't adapt.]

"I don't know."

And then we were playing The Staring Game. There was something behind Abram's eyes I'd not seen in all the years we'd been married. Now I was more than a little uncomfortable. I blinked.

"Very funny, Abram," I forced a soft chuckle. [His jokes were usually funnier than this].

"I'm not joking."

The Staring Game, Round Two. I thought I'd check to make sure I understood.

"So you and some of the herdsmen are going on a boys' trip?"

Silence.

"You and I are going out for a few days of private relaxation?"

Silence, and staring.

"Who will we leave behind to tend our household and your business while we're gone?"

Silence, deep breath, and a blink.

I began to comprehend the words that were coming out of his mouth.

"We're moving west, as in toward the edge of the world where people disappear, and we're taking everyone—all our possessions, all our herdsmen and their families, our business, our <u>future</u>—but you don't know how far west or how long this trip will take. Is that what you're telling me?"

"Yes."

Four thousand years ago, we had no Travel Channel, no public television documentaries, not even a map or a postcard to tell us what lay beyond the western horizon where the sun disappeared every day. All we had were stories of people who'd traveled that direction and never come back. It was common knowledge that at some point west the world ended and unlucky travelers fell off into...well, no one had come back to tell us what they fell into. I blinked again.

"Okay, Abram. Enough mystery. What's going on?"

Now, I know the next words he spoke are some of the most monumental in the history of forever, but when I heard them there was no way I could understand their significance. I believed in a world ruled by many gods, not One Supreme Deity. I'd never heard of Yahweh. I'd certainly never heard of a Savior Messiah whose lineage would trace directly back to this conversation. There was no Bible to reference, no cultural backdrop, no historical experience of any kind to help me comprehend Abram's next words.

"God spoke to me. He promised to bless me and the whole world through me. He promised I will be the father of a great nation, but first we have to leave here and follow Him until we get to the land He's giving us. He hasn't told me where it is, but He'll tell us when to stop."[10]

"A god spoke to you?" [No god had ever spoken to me or to anyone I knew, but a god-spoken journey was something I could get on board with.] "Which god? Our moon god Nanna? You know I used to pray to him for a child. He finally speaks and it's to you? Well, at least I know he's not deaf and mute."

"No, not Nanna."

"Who then? Utu? Inanna? Ninhursag?" [As I said, we had many gods in those days.[11]]

"Not any god we've heard of. Actually, I don't know His name, but I know He's God."

Sitting on that cushion hearing my 75-year-old husband tell me we were leaving civilization to disappear into the unknown because the disembodied Voice of an unnamed, unknown deity told him he was going to be father of anything at all, much less "a great nation," you'd maybe expect me to be extremely skeptical, maybe even a little angry. If he wasn't Abram and I wasn't Sarai, maybe, but we were partners. Perhaps having been childless all our lives had forced a bond strong enough to face the edge of the world together. Perhaps it was the depth of that look in his eyes or the certainty in his words. For whatever reason, in that moment I believed in a Voice I'd never heard. I nodded.

"When do we leave?"

"As soon as we're packed."

There was no freshly baked barley bread that night. I immediately began rounding up the servants, giving them assignments. I sent word to Lot's household to do the same. The next days were a whirlwind. We weren't stuffing a few changes of clothing into a knapsack and throwing a carry-on over a donkey's back. Abram and I had accumulated considerable wealth in our many years, in the way of people, livestock, and substance, and we'd need it all when we reached the mysterious land of the mysterious Voice.

WORTH CHASING

Abram and I had had our share of adventures, but nothing like the one upon which we now embarked. We'd followed the banks of the Euphrates River 600 miles north when we made the move from Ur to Haran. There were small settlements along the river and we'd found life in Haran similar to life in Ur, on a less metropolitan scale. This new journey was into a vast unknown emptiness. West of Haran were thousands of square miles of sand and then—well, that remained to be discovered.

There were no roads, no maps, or anyone to ask for directions. Of course, roads, maps, and directions would only have been useful if we knew where we were going. We didn't. We set out across an endless ocean of sand with only our belief in The Promise of a God Whose name we didn't know leading the way. In case you're wondering, Abram's mystery Voice wasn't speaking every day. Only Abram heard The Voice. He heard it once; we packed and left. Now there was no Voice. There was just sand, sun, and heading toward the edge of the world, day after long, hot day.

At 65 years old, you'd probably expect my journey was nearing its end. Truthfully, I assumed I'd live the rest of my life in Haran, growing old and rich with Abram. I could not conceive that Abram and I would walk the most exciting and important paths in a land we'd never imagined, following a God we'd never heard of.

We traveled every sandy mile side by side. We gazed hopefully—sometimes frightfully—into every shadowy tomorrow, made every good or bad choice, and reaped every blessing or consequence *together*. That's what happens in marriage, everything that happens to your husband also happens to you—and in case you haven't experienced it yet, that sandstorm blows both ways.

Abram received The Promise; together we believed The Promise. If Abram was to be a father, Sarai was to be a mother. Some things were different in those days, but even in Sumer, men weren't having babies, so children for him must mean children for me. After a life defined by childlessness, that was a promise worth chasing, even chasing across thousands of miles of mystery toward the edge of the world.

Promises are powerful. They incite us to things we'd never consider outside their power. Within days of our conversation, I was looking over my shoulder at Haran for the last time. Together, Abram and I were chasing a promise.

HANGING OUT IN THE HAREM

Abram's words echoed in my thoughts as I stared toward the horizon those first weeks in the desert: "Father of a great nation. Father of a great nation. Father of a great nation." Mother of a great nation? For the first time in 20 years, I had hope.

Lest you think otherwise, there is no difference between a year in your day and a year in mine. There's no such thing as "Bible years." Four thousand years ago a year was 365 days, just as it is now. I lived 365 24-hour days every year, just as you do, and was 65 in exactly the same way you will one day be 65, if you're not already. My body was no different from other women's; it had been many years since it had given any indication it could bring forth a child.

Still, the passion I saw in Abram's eyes and heard in his voice as he told me of The Voice and its Promise inspired me to hope. Many nights during those first months, I would lie in the silence of our tent and picture myself gazing into the face of our child. He'd look like Abram, but have my eyes. Or I'd stare into the darkness and imagine what my childhood friends back in Ur might say if they ever heard Abram and I had a child. *"Did you hear about Sarai and Abram? Finally! And at her age!"* How they would laugh! Such thoughts made me smile broadly into the star-filled night. Hope felt good!

Sometimes I'd ponder what I would name our son, and narrowed the list to three I thought Abram might approve: Jokshan, Midian, and Shuah. I'd fall asleep and dream of the happy days ahead when I would finally have a child. Every morning I awoke full of confidence that today would be the day we'd reach the land of The Promise. Every night I closed my eyes knowing in the morning we'd set out again. Maybe tomorrow.

HOME SWEET HOME

I don't know how many tomorrows passed before we reached Canaan. On a good day, our sprawling caravan of livestock and people crawled about eight miles.[12] That's per day, not per hour. Some days sandstorms immobilized us completely. After several months, we turned south to follow the base of a long mountain range. We passed through the city of Damascus and finally crossed into Canaan. It was in Shechem of Canaan that The God, who until now had been a One-Hit-Wonder Voice in the darkness, appeared to Abram and told him he was standing on the land our descendants would inherit.[13]

My heart danced when Abram told me we'd finally reached our new home. Not only had we not fallen off the edge off the world, Canaan was a beautiful place to raise a child. Bounded on the east by the Jordan River and on the west by The Great Sea,[14] it was a land to be desired. It was also a land currently occupied. The Canaanites would have taken exception to Abram declaring himself the new owner of such great real estate, so Abram built a rock altar at the spot he'd met with The God and we continued south, deeper into our new land in search of a stopping point.

As it turned out, we wouldn't be stopping long in Canaan. We camped about two weeks' journey south of Shechem, near Bethel. After a time, we realized there wasn't enough food available to sustain a band of nomads as large as ours. Apparently, the climate often changed drastically from year to year in our new country, and we arrived in the middle of a drought-induced famine.

Hearing stories of a vast kingdom built along the banks of a mighty river that sounded much like the Euphrates, we headed west again. Where there was water, there was food. More notably to my still-a-city-girl's mind, where there was a vast kingdom, there was a bazaar, and where there was a bazaar, there were clothes, jewelry, rugs, clothes, jewelry, blankets, clothes, jewelry and pottery—did I say clothes and jewelry? Apparently, the materialism of my upbringing had made the trip with me across all those miles of sand. I'd grown weary of my once favorite robes, belts, and veils and longed for new finery.

DANGEROUS BEAUTY

Always moving as we did from place to place with no shelter but the walls of our goat hair tents[15] was dangerous, and we'd wisely avoided other people when we could. So far on our trip from Haran we'd come across a few clans not completely unlike us; some even spoke languages similar to ours. The Amorites were nomads who roamed west and south of Haran. We'd stayed out of their path as much as possible as their tribal chiefs had a reputation for hostility.[16] The Canaanites we met near Shechem were more established and lived in small market towns where they grew food and kept livestock.[17] They were less aggressive than the Amorites, but still, we kept our distance.

If the stories of the wealthy kingdom in the west were true, now we were purposely heading into a land densely populated by people we knew nothing about. Knowing there was no way to avoid contact with these strange people in their strange land magnified our awareness of our vulnerability.

Living in a mud-brick house in a city surrounded by family and friends and governed by laws to protect people and property, beauty can be a blessing. Traveling through a wilderness moving always closer to the edge of the world, never knowing what kind of people you might run into in that vast wilderness, beauty is a burden. Walking willfully into a foreign country rumored to be ruled by men who believed they were gods, beauty was a hazard, and frankly, I was dangerously beautiful, even in my later years.

My green eyes and still-onyx-black hair had always set me apart from other women in Sumer, but Abram said my smile was the real beguilement. In the ancient world, straight, white teeth like mine were even more uncommon than my eyes. As a child, my mother instructed me to pay special homage to Inanna, the Sumerian goddess of beauty and desire,[18] for my sparkling eyes and captivating smile. Inanna was also a goddess of fertility.[19] Eyes the color of cypress leaves and a smile as bright as our finest gem-smith's crystals were small consolation for barrenness. Gratitude for my looks turned to resentment early in life as I began to believe my beauty was cruel mockery of my overshadowing insufficiency. Regardless how beautiful the engravings, an urn that won't hold water is just… pretty.

MAKING MONEY IN EGYPT

Abram was brave, brave enough to stare across countless miles of desert to where the sky touched the earth and walk boldly toward that falling-off point every day. He was also caring and faithful. We had a perfectly balanced relationship, and Abram looked to me for wisdom and insight throughout our lives together.[20]

No, that wasn't the custom in all marriages four thousand years ago, but neither was leaving your home and everything you'd ever known in response to the call of a Voice from the sky. Our marriage was different; it had to be for us to walk the roadless desert through which we now traveled. My unique position in our household meant I always had a say in important matters [21]—such as if I was going to call myself Abram's wife or sister.

If you've heard this next part of my story and picked up that Abram was somehow hiding behind me or betraying me, please put that thought down, because this is how I recall the conversation:

Two nights before we reached Egypt, Abram and I were in our tent, strategizing what we would do when we reached the land of the river and met its people.[22] *We agreed the first thing we'd do was give the ruler of the country some of our livestock, people, and if need be, even some of my jewelry, as payment for letting us wait out Canaan's famine. That plan established, we had to talk about the camel in the tent.*

"Sarai, there's no way for you to avoid being seen once we reach the land along the river. We both know you're beautiful and there's a real possibility some man may see you and want you to be his wife."

"I've been thinking about that, too. Keeping to our tent when people were around has been fine so

far, but if we're going to be there long, hiding isn't going to work. Depending how hostile they are, they might actually kill you if they know you're my husband. If that happens, there's no way for us to accomplish what The God has said, and we'll have come all this way for nothing."

"You're right. I think we have two options. We can turn around and go back to Canaan, but there's no food there and we and all our people and livestock might starve. Or if a man sees you and wants you, we can tell him you're my sister, not my wife, and he won't have any reason to kill me."

"That's exactly what I was thinking! After all, you are my half-brother. And Abram, I don't know if you've thought this through as thoroughly as I have, but as my brother not only will they not kill you, depending on how wealthy they are, they'll probably pay you a sizeable dowry for me." [I'd heard these people were very wealthy].

It was dark in the tent. I couldn't see Abram's face, but I knew his silence meant he was calculating the financial benefits of the plan. After a few minutes of silence, he responded.

"I hadn't thought of that, but you're probably right. Good-night, Sis."

He was always trying to make me laugh.

A few days after our caravan rambled into Egypt, I made my way to one of the bazaars. The light colored, tight fitting clothing and heavy jewelry the women wore captivated me. I went on a bit of a spree, buying handfuls of veils, more than a dozen lightweight linen robes for myself and as many for Abram. I avoided counting how many pieces of Egyptian jewelry I piled in my handmaid's basket. My extravagance turned the heads of women in the market as much as my beauty turned the heads of the men. I was not trying to attract attention, but looking back my reckless spending probably was unwise.

Not a surprise, the next day a messenger came from Pharaoh asking about me. Abram and I stuck to our story that I was his younger, unattached sister. Almost immediately, I was ushered into the palace as part of Pharaoh's harem. As we hoped, in return Pharaoh sent Abram a fortune in silver, gold, sheep, cattle, and camels, as well as male and female donkeys and male and female servants. "Male and female" meant not only had our wealth grown substantially, it would continue to grow exponentially.

WORSE THAN DEATH

Remember when I told Abram I'd thought this scheme through "thoroughly"? It took me only a few minutes of hanging out in the harem to realize with terrifying clarity

I had not. Our wealth may have doubled overnight and Abram's life was saved, but I was on my way to becoming Wife Number I-Don't-Know-How-Many of the Pharaoh of Egypt. Once a wife of Pharaoh, always a wife of Pharaoh. This was a life sentence worse than a death sentence.

My days of promise chasing were over. I had entered deliberately into a palatial prison, relinquishing my freedom, my hope, my dignity, and my place at Abram's side. Separated from Abram forever, he would be forced to take a new wife so he could fulfill The Promise of The God. He would travel back to Canaan in the agonizing knowledge that I was living my days in dark deceit waiting to die in secret shame in this strange land.

What had we done?

Abram and I didn't see that our perfect plan was a treacherous trap until it was too late. I don't know you, but I'd venture you may have found yourself trapped in a "harem" of your own at some point—maybe more than once. Such harems are the typical destination of self-determined journeys.

You see, The God did not tell Abram to travel to Egypt. The God told him Canaan was his new home. Fearing the famine, Abram and I reasoned we could more easily provide for ourselves and for those under our care in a foreign land. We knew there would be danger and determined to protect ourselves against that danger through deceit. Our misguided attempt at self-provision and self-protection landed me in a luxurious cage and caused Abram indescribable emotional anguish.

THE WAY OUT

Abram and I clearly did not know Who we were following. We could not trust One we didn't yet know, and we could not know One we had not yet experienced. Much of the trouble, turmoil, or difficulty we find ourselves in is because we don't trust the One in control of our journey so we take the camel's bridle into our own hands. That was true for Abram and I just as it's true for you.

You know you've tripped and fallen into the harem when you blink and think "Oh, no! What have I done?" It's the tent you share with Regret and Fear as you wait in anguish to get what you deserve. It's the dark holding pen of impending consequence; the brink of Something Else, not the verge of Something Great.

There is a way out of Pharaoh's harem, but it's not a hasty exit. Hasty exits from harems don't lead out to freedom. They are trapdoors disguised as exits leading to deeper, darker corridors to yet another holding pen of dread. The only way to get safely out the harem is to dig in and wait.

I know "wait" is an ugly word and digging in is the last thing you want to do in the middle of your "What have I done?", but waiting is the way out. God can't bless your plans when you've taken the reins and willfully ridden down a path He never intended you to follow, but He will sustain you as you wait in stillness for His promise, even in a harem of your own making.

In your English language when you say "wait" it implies a pause, a time of doing nothing but watching the sun come up and go down. In Hebrew, we have different words for "wait." So that you can better understand what I mean when I say you have to wait to escape the harem, let me explain.

In your Book of Psalms (how I wish I'd had those songs when I was wandering in the wilderness!), the writer encourages you that no one who waits on God will ever be ashamed (Psalm 25:3). Where your text says just "wait," I would say the Hebrew word *qavah*, which means to bind together as you would twist two cords.[23] It's not a do-nothing time. To *qavah* is deliberate. It's an act of strengthening, as two cords twisted tightly together are stronger than two cords simply hung side by side. It's an act of joining yourself to the One on Whom you wait, as you purposefully bind your heart to Him.

The prophet Habakkuk wrote a nice little book in which he could have been speaking directly to me in my situation. He said, "For the vision is yet for the appointed time; it hastens toward the goal and it will not fail. Though it tarries, wait for it; for it will certainly come, it will not delay" (Habakkuk 2:3 NASB). There the word used is *chakah*, which means, "to adhere to," and is related to the word *chaqah,* which means, "to dig in and prepare."[24] Again, this is not an instruction to pass the time absentmindedly. It's a time of getting ready for the Something Great just outside the harem tent flap.

Waiting binds you to God as you dig in and prepare to receive all He has promised. Holding fast, you get to know Him. More than anything, He wants you to know Him because when you know Him, you will trust Him, and where there is trust there is relationship. It's pressing in and waiting that ultimately produces the character to sustain the relationship to which God's called you. As dire as hanging out in the harem is, it's there you often begin to experience His sovereignty.

Of course, I didn't know any of this as I languished in despair dreading the moment the eunuchs would come and lead me into Pharaoh's private quarters. More than a decade would pass before I understood my time in the harem was the beginning of getting to know The God.

Thankfully, there was a purification period between when a woman became part of Pharaoh's harem and when she officially and everlastingly became his wife. Not long after my arrival in the harem, everyone in the palace became very sick. Pharaoh somehow discerned I was the cause of the plague and summoned Abram and me to his throne. It was a very short conversation.

> *"What have you done? Why didn't you tell me she was your wife? Why did you say, 'She's my sister,' so that I took her for my wife? Now then, here is your wife; take your wife and go!"*[25]

Our time in Egypt was much shorter than anticipated. Armed men escorted us immediately out of the country with all our belongings; everything we had when we arrived **and** everything Pharaoh had given us.

HOW?

Leaving Egypt so abruptly, I struggled to understand what was happening: I was spared a life of shame and despair. Abram was spared the pain and humiliation of knowing I was living in secret disgrace as Pharaoh's wife. Even Pharaoh was spared the consequences he and his kingdom surely would have reaped had he taken me for his wife. Abram and I were together. Our wealth had grown exponentially. The Promise was not lost.

How was any of this possible? How did Pharaoh know I was Abram's wife? Even if someone told him, why would he think I was the cause of the plague in his house and let me go? Why would he let Abram keep the dowry? For that matter, why would he let Abram keep his life after such deceit?

This was not the way of the world as I knew it. What sort of journey were we on? What manner of god were we following? It would take time, but all my questions would be answered.

THE COVENANT AND THE COMPROMISE

Wandering again through the desert east of Egypt, we were no longer a caravan; we were a traveling town. There were more than 200 men in our company, and I'd lost count of the women and children as that number seemed to increase almost weekly. Our herds of oxen, sheep, camels, and donkeys stretched around us as far as we could see. Many miles ago in Haran when The Voice promised to bless Abram, of course our Sumerian minds assumed that meant wealth but never dreamed of riches of this magnitude.

The famine hadn't relented when we returned to Canaan, and ample pastureland and food for herds and households as large as ours were hard to find. Lot made the trip to Egypt and back with us. His flocks and people also were increasing, so returning to the scarcity of Canaan, quarrels began between his herdsmen and ours over whose animals would graze which pastures.

To end the conflict, Abram, who was always more softhearted than prudent when it came to our nephew, let Lot choose which part of our new country he wanted.

Lot chose the green valley land to the east along the Jordan River. (I always said he was a smart boy!). Abram and I traveled into the more-brown-than-green hilly desert and settled near a grove of large oak trees about two miles from a fledgling settlement that later became the city of Hebron.[26] The trees were on the property of an Amorite named Mamre, whom Abram befriended.[27]

DYING DREAMS

It was pleasant land, even if it wasn't as lush as the valley where Lot now lived. Looking back, I should have been more grateful for such beautiful land and those towering oaks, but somewhere between Haran and that grove, my heart wandered off behind a sand dune and never came back. It didn't go alone. It took my dying dreams and the last remnants of my imagination with it.

Imagination isn't a childish pastime; neither is it the opposite of reality. Imagination is the capacity to create a reality beyond what you experience with your senses, which makes it essential to faith. Faith requires seeing with your heart what is invisible to your eye and living as though the invisible is tangible. Imagination stretches beyond your intellect so that it influences not only your mind but also your will and emotions and allows you to conceive the inconceivable. And there was the problem. Imagination requires the one ability I did not possess, the ability to conceive.

Few things strike at the core of a woman's identity as glaringly as the inability to conceive. We are the ones who cradle life in our bodies. We are the ones who nurture life and bring it to be, whether that life grows inside us or we take it into our hearts. We give it milk, cover it up at night, and raise it into its place. Women are the ones who help it stand on its own two feet so one day it can walk off into The Promise itself. Sometimes it's people; sometimes dreams, visions, even ministries. It's part of our original design. At least it's supposed to be.

I'd lived a lifetime unable to conceive, and not just in the physical. Barrenness wasn't only a condition of my body. The inability of my body to allow anything to take root and grow was a reflection of the same inability of my mind. There was no promise coming, no belly bump of hope. I was convinced of the reality of the Voice, the existence of this new-but-nameless God, but the reality of His promise to me was dangling over the edge.

Yes, I heard The Promise from Abram. Yes, I traveled across the desert with him. Yes, I believed—for a time, until reality reminded me who I was. I had always been and would always be Sarai the Barren. That reality, branded into the flesh of my heart, was confirmed by a lifetime of irrefutable evidence. The Promise would not—could not—take root. My mind was an inhospitable environment for hope and faith to live.

THE STING OF DISAPPOINTMENT

Imagination starves to death on a diet of reality substantiated by score keeping. As well as I can recall, I'd started keeping score somewhere around our time near Bethel. In my mind, I'd chiseled out a column for "Days of Promise Kept" versus "Days of Promise Not Kept". So far, there were no tally marks in the "Promise Kept" column, and I had grown weary of waiting.

I had no *Book of Psalms* to turn to for hope or insight. The author of those great words of encouragement wouldn't be born for 600 years. Neither was the Prophet Habakkuk around to cheer me on to dig in and hold on to The Far-Too-Slowly-Manifesting Promise of the Mysterious No-Named God Abram so willingly ran after. I was old, I'd grown tired, and I'd had my fill of shattered hopes.

The sting of disappointment I lived with month after month gave me no comfort or reason to continue clinging to The Promise of a God with no name, Who in my mind was no more able to answer my pleas for a child than the deaf gods whose wooden idols I'd bowed to back in Sumer. I'd left Haran in a flurry of fanciful thinking, feeding my dreams promises from a Voice in the sky, imagining myself holding a child with Abram's strong jaw and my green eyes. It didn't take too many months of walking in circles in a wasteland to realize how irrational I'd been.

What a fool I must have seemed to the younger women in our company, trekking across this wasteland, believing at my age some mysterious God could somehow give me a child. I was sure they were mocking me behind my back. Wisely, they'd so far kept their ridicule to themselves.

Facing the truth, I understood now The Promise was for Abram, and I chose to believe it *for him*. Any notion that such a miracle included me was nonsense. Settling into our encampment near the oak trees, I chose to feast on facts rather than fantasy. The facts were I had begun this journey as barren as the land through which we traveled and these years of waiting had changed nothing.

My fanciful wilderness heart song of "The Promise is coming! The Promise is coming!" was being drowned out by the lament of my days back in Haran, "You are barren. You are barren. You are *barren*." Every empty-armed day hardened my mind. Day by day I silenced the voice of hope I'd foolishly let speak to my heart those early months. It wasn't long before it was nothing more than a muffled, gasping whisper.

NOW WHAT?

One night after we'd been living near the oak grove for several years, Abram didn't come home. He'd spent other nights out, when checking our herds had taken him more than a half-day's journey away, but this night was alarmingly dark. The stars in the moonless sky seemed dim and distant; I was uneasy. I'd fallen asleep in the great darkness more than a little concerned at his absence and dreamed a dream I'd not had in years.

It was a dream I used to have at the beginning of our journey, when I'd fall asleep thinking of names for our son. In the dream, I would be staring in wonder at my round stomach, then I'd awaken suddenly and quickly place my hand on my still-flat, empty womb. I endured the cruelty of waking from such dreams for many years. After a time, they became the nightmares I dreaded.

When I awoke from the nightmare the next morning, Abram was standing over me, his hands covered in what looked like dried blood and sand. I sat up with a start.

"Ick! What do you have all over you? And where were you last night? I was worried."

"It's blood. I should've washed up a bit. I probably look a mess."

"Well, yes, you do. How did you get so much blood on you? It's up past your elbows."

"I was out last night cutting a covenant with God."

I had just started rolling up my sleeping mat, but stopped mid-roll. I took a deep breath and turned my head up to meet his eyes, almost dreading what

THE COVENANT AND THE COMPROMISE | 51

I might see. There it was, that same look I'd seen all those years ago in Haran.

Ten years I'd lived in this tent, in this wasteland. Ten years of waiting. Ten years of nothing happening. Ten years of watching my already-old, barren body shrivel in the desert heat. Ten years of no baby. Ten years of disappointment. Ten years! Now what? I tried to mask the skepticism in my tone.

"The same God who told you you were going to be a father, or is this a new god?"

Unmoved by my cynicism, he nodded eagerly. "He said He's the same God who brought us out of Ur, out of Haran to give us this land of Canaan. He said He was going to be a shield to protect me and that He was going to give me a great reward!"[28]

[His excitement was irritating.]

"And you and The God now have a contract or blood covenant of some sort?" [Careful with your tone. Your name is showing.]

I knew about cutting covenants or contracts from our business dealings. Animals were cut in half and their halved carcasses placed on the ground where the blood could pool between them.

Parties to the contract stood on opposite ends of the bloody walkway and then walked through the blood between the body halves, exchanging sides. As they did this, they recited the terms of their agreement. The blood represented how serious each party was about keeping their end of the deal.[29]

"Well, I actually fell asleep before the covenant was completed, but I did gather the animals, cut them in half and lay them out on the ground. I had to keep chasing the vultures away until dark. Once the sun went down, it was so dark I fell asleep. While I was sleeping, God walked between the bodies of the animals and told me He's going to bless me and my descendants **forever***!"*

I looked at Abram's feet. They were sandy, but otherwise clean. I took a silent breath and paced my words, still struggling to temper my sarcasm.

"Okay. So what really happened is you didn't actually walk the covenant, The God walked it, and as He did, He told you all these wonderful things He will make happen for you?"

"Yes! He said 'descendants,' Sarai! Descendants!"

"Mmmm. I see."

I thought about ending the conversation there. I was tired of this "insider" telling me—the obvious "outsider"—all the wonderful things The Voice said. I should have kept silent. I couldn't.

"And you believe this God and trust His covenant, even though you didn't actually **do** *anything? I mean, it seems to me The God did all the real covenant making. That's not usually how these things work. Since you were sleeping, you really don't have a valid claim on Him to fulfill any of the wonderful promises He made. Legally speaking, that is." [My tone grew icier by the syllable.]*

"Yes, I believe Him! Absolutely! He's not like the gods we worshipped in Sumer. He's—well, He's God. And yes, I know that's not how covenants usually work, Sarai, but seriously, nothing about any of this has been usual. I can't explain why, but I **know** *He will do everything He said."*

I stood and stared into his eyes without speaking. I could tell my prolonged silence was making him uncomfortable. In truth, I sort of enjoyed his discomfort so I bit my tongue before it got away from me and started a real argument, one I'd be obligated to sustain. He continued:

"What I **know** *is God walked through the blood while I slept and told me my descendants would*

be as countless as the stars in the sky. He said they'd endure some trials, even be enslaved in a foreign country for a time, but in the end, the land we're now living in will be theirs forever. And not just here, but from the river in Egypt all the way to the Euphrates in Sumer."

"Did you happen to mention to this real God the small but important detail that you don't have any children?" [There was no way he could miss the cynicism in that.]

"Yes! And this is the best part, the part I've been trying to get to! I suggested to God naming Eliezer my heir, as we've raised him in our house since we acquired his mother so long ago in Damascus, but God said no. His exact words were, 'One who will come forth from your own body, he shall be your heir.'[30] *From me, Sarai! A child of my own! I am going to be a father!"*

He looked at me, his eyes brimming tears of joy, breathless with the excitement of his last words.

A knot started forming in my stomach. I'd dreaded this day for years; the day I would let Abram know I wasn't going to be the mother of his child. What else could I do? It was obvious I was never going to conceive. Abram and I had tried for a decade since hearing The Promise (not to mention many decades before). I'd known for years The Promise wasn't for me; now I had to tell Abram.

Neither of us spoke: Abram because he was out of breath, me because the dread had worked its way from my stomach into my throat. As soon as I was able, I broke the silence.

"I don't know if you've noticed, but apparently The God hasn't included me in His promise to you. It's been ten years, Abram. I'm 75. Seventy-five! I'm not having any babies. Those days are long past. But I've been thinking about this for a while, and I have a plan."

[An echo from the past!]

"We've given The God more than enough time to fulfill His Promise, and He's done nothing. Well, not really nothing: He's consistently prevented me from conceiving. Your meeting with Him last night confirms what I've been thinking, that **we** *need to do something to fulfill this Promise. I think that 'some<u>thing</u>' might be some<u>one</u>."*

I had to stop and steel myself for what I was about to say. I exhaled and just let my brain and tongue overrun my heart as the next words tumbled out like spilled wheat on the desert sand.

"I want you to take Hagar, my Egyptian servant, as another wife. She's young; maybe she'll be able to give you a child. It's too late for me, but maybe not for you."

There. It was said. Let Abram have his child with Hagar. I was done with The Promise and the pain of continual disappointment. My shoulders sagged almost imperceptibly as a wave of hollow relief washed over me.

I took a deep breath, straightened my shoulders, and knelt back down to finish rolling up my bed mat, my back to Abram. I couldn't look at him, and I wanted—no, needed—this conversation to stop. There was nothing more to say. I busied myself with nothing, really; our tent wasn't that big.

I couldn't see Abram's face, but I could feel his jubilance about the fresh covenant and his very real, very tangible encounter with The God running out like water from a broken urn. I could hear him breathing, slowly and deliberately. After a few minutes, I turned to invite a response, if he had any. I was ready.

He was gone.

I wasn't ready for that.

Alone with my thoughts, I comforted myself by commending my wisdom, even my selflessness in helping provide a child for Abram. Ten years of waiting as a nomad in a foreign land made it clear nothing was going to happen unless I made it happen.

Apparently, whatever plan The God had in the beginning had not worked out, and it was now up to me to make sure Abram had his son. Yes, my plan was a good plan, a plan that would work. The God either wouldn't or couldn't give me a child, but I could still assure Abram an heir, even if it meant sharing my husband with another woman. I gave up my most cherished position as his only wife, so Abram could have a child and thus fulfill The God's promise.

The dark dread of the night before was sunshine delight compared to the horror that settled over me that night, as I lay alone in our tent. Abram had gone to Hagar's tent, as I'd instructed. For 60 years, I'd been Abram's wife, his only wife. Others we knew had multiple wives, but Abram always said I was enough for him, despite my famous deficiency and infamous disposition. He'd never seemed even the slightest bit interested in the idea before, but The Promise from The God had changed everything—again. I wasn't enough, I never would be, and now, I feared, Abram agreed.

ALONE IN THE DARK

He could have said no.

No one knew my husband as I did: knew by heart the calloused spots on his hands, knew about the scar under his left arm where an ox gored him 50 years ago, or knew his beard, so coarse around his mouth, was fine and smooth under his chin. *He could have said no.*

Hagar's tent was no more than 50 feet from where I lay, alone in the dark, listening to the sound of my shallow breathing, feeling each explosive beat of my heart scream into the shadows, "Come back! Come back! Come back! Come back!" *He could have said no.*

It was too late. He was with her. He wasn't coming back and we would never be the same. I buried my head in my cushion to strangle the jagged sobs as the black emptiness of my tent swallowed me. What had I done?

Why didn't he say no?

THE COUNTERFEIT AND THE COST

Within weeks, everyone knew Hagar had conceived. She made sure of it. I wish I could tell you I rejoiced with Abram upon hearing the news. I wish I could say Hagar looked to me as a respected mentor and that I considered her the bearer of a beautiful gift. You've traveled this far because you want the story as I lived it, so I can tell you none of those lies.

Hagar's pregnancy was the deathblow to my failing hope. Until now, Abram's ability to father a child had been untested. If Hagar did not conceive, it meant maybe I wasn't the problem—or at least not the only problem. The report of Hagar's condition confirmed for Abram and the rest of our world that I was, in fact, the cause of our childlessness; the beautiful, empty urn. My hope took its last labored breath.

Hope is the confident expectation that something good is waiting for you beyond the horizon where the desert meets the sky. It's the wonder that beckons you and the power that propels you. Hope produces the joy and strength you need to sustain you through times of waiting. Without hope, waiting is a prison of monotony: The days are perpetually hot and dry, the horizon promises only more sand, and the poison of jealousy saturates and distorts your mind.

Jealousy is born when hope dies because without hope, you begrudge even the tiniest blessing in the lives of others. Jealousy is the reaction you have when you see something alive in someone that is dead in you. It's the black ice that fills your soul while at the same time magnifying your emptiness. It breeds discontentment, anger, and spiteful resentment.

ALL I COULD TAKE

Evidence of Hagar's pregnancy was quick to appear; too quick, in my opinion. I suspected her of padding her stomach under her robes so she could more easily flaunt her position as the expectant mother of Abram's child. Devoid of hope, I became viciously jealous of Hagar. Hagar could conceive. Hagar could nurture life. Hagar could do what I would never do: She could give my husband a child.

For her part, Hagar had no reservations about parading her round figure for me at every opportunity. As much as I envied and resented Hagar, she despised me.[31] Her haughtiness toward and scorn for me were no secret to any in our household. One day, after I'd had all I could take of her arrogance, I began to rail against her to Abram.

"Do you not see how Hagar is treating me? She barely acknowledges when I speak to her, and responds with nothing but that arrogant smirk she wears day and night. She struts between our tent and hers, entering our tent without even asking permission. And I know she's gossiping to the other women about us. I've had all I can take of her. You need to do something!"

"Hold on, Sarai. Why do I need to do something?"

"Because it's your fault she's treating me so badly."

*"How exactly is this **my** fault?"*

"Because she's expecting your child, that's how."

*"Okay, you seem to be forgetting Hagar was your idea, not mine. Taking another wife never occurred to me. That was **your** plan, Sarai. I just went along with it."*

With piercing clarity, I remembered Abram's silence as I rolled my bed mat that morning in our tent. I swallowed the words, "You could have said 'no'!" before I regretted them forever, but he was right. This fiasco was my plan, although it seemed a moment of brilliance when I'd thought of it. I thought it would be easy. I thought it was the perfect solution. Now the whole mess enraged me. I was too angry to speak, almost trembling with fury.

*"You also seem to be forgetting that wife or not, baby or not, Hagar is still **your** maid. She still works for **you**. You have authority over our household. If you think something needs doing, do what seems right to **you**."[32]*

He walked away before I could recover enough composure to respond. In all our years of marriage, we'd never had a more confrontational conversation. I laid the blame for the chasm growing between Abram and me directly in Hagar's disappearing lap.

I'm sure I don't have to tell you that even in her arrogance Hagar was not the problem. Abram obviously was not the problem. My cruel reaction to Hagar erupted out of my jealousy for her condition, but that amount of fury doesn't happen in a few months' time.

My anger began as a slow simmer way back in Ur, controllable and quiet, as I watched my friends have baby after baby, heir after heir, while I kept folding then refolding clean blankets and storing them in an empty bassinette. I kept the lid on my simmer, eventually convincing myself that Abram was enough and we had so much together that babies didn't matter. Then my friends' children began having children and my simmer rolled up, concealed (so I thought) behind ornate veils and sparkling jewelry.

Watching the effects of time on my aging body actually cooled the searing heat of perpetual disappointment as the realities of biology ruled out even the possibility of a child. Exhausted resignation finally replaced my seething. Then **this**! The God with The Voice makes a promise that touches me all the way to my heartbreak and promises to heal the most secret place of my hurt. ***And I believed it***!

Of course, nothing happened. Nothing. Well, not exactly nothing. I was watching yet another belly grow, and it wasn't mine—*again.* But it *was* my husband's child and heir, the one I wanted, the one I so longed for. There wasn't enough cold water or self-control on earth to stop that raging boil.

In truth, seeing Hagar's condition merely gave me a target at which to direct my rage. The frighteningly fierce fire I now barely contained ignited under the scorching heat of the desert we'd trudged through and had smoldered for years in the empty space where my heart once lived. Somewhere along the journey, my heart, weary of waiting on what now seemed an empty Promise, had wandered away from the Promise Maker. I'd supposed it died behind some nondescript sand dune. I never bothered to go look for it.

DEAD FAITH

There's a verse in your Bible that admonishes you not to let your heart get lost along the journey. Galatians 6:9 says "Let us not grow weary in well doing, for in due time we will reap a harvest, if we do not give up." The words translated "grow weary" are from the Greek *egkakeó*, which means, "to lose heart."[33] The apostle who wrote those words to you had been on many journeys. He understood that growing weary of well doing could happen to any of us at one time or another, especially when we are waiting; waiting for a breakthrough, for a promise to be fulfilled, for a new start, for a refreshing breath.

Hearts get lost when waiting does not produce the result we desire, and I had waited well beyond what I believed was reasonable for The God to keep His Promise. The great adventure Abram and I had embarked upon had become a never-ending torment of one disappointing day after another. More than ten years had passed and there was no child. Nothing had been born, but something surely had died.

When your heart wanders off, taking your imagination and crippling your hope, your faith dies. A lost heart and a dead faith exact a heavy price, on you and those around you. I blamed everyone for not following the script as I wrote it in my now-dead imagination. I remembered with private shame the early days of our journey, when I would foolishly dream of myself pregnant, imagining how it would feel to carry a ballooning future, laying our baby in Abram's nervous arms, nursing the child, teaching him to walk, talk, obey, succeed. Those memories now humiliated and enraged me.

I had it all worked out, and now I blamed The God for preventing me from conceiving. I blamed Abram for Hagar's pregnancy. I blamed Hagar for the ever-widening gulf between Abram and me. There was blame enough for everyone to share and I was meting it out eagerly and generously. Everybody was blamed—everybody but me.

As he pointed out, Abram had nothing to do with concocting the plan that resulted in the torment I now endured. It wasn't a moment of weakness or desire that sent him to Hagar's tent. It was *me*. He went because he trusted *me*. He trusted my wisdom that, up until now, had been trustworthy. He trusted my devotion to him. He trusted my creativity and my intelligence and my insight. He had no way of knowing how distorted my judgment had become in the absence of my heart.

PLAYING GOD

As destructive as blaming others is, the most dangerous path a wandering heart takes is down the Road of Compromise. Dead faith is the gateway to the Road to Compromise as you choose your own way, your own solution, your own scheme over the plan of the Promise Maker. Put another way, dead faith leads to playing God.

Your Bible says that God will not share His glory with another.[34] That "another" includes you just as it included me. God created us to seek relationship with Him and follow His roads. He knows the way. There's never a time He needs our help. I did not understand that. For all my wit and wisdom and savvy and spunk, I just did not understand.

After blaming The God for preventing me from conceiving, I took control and played God to salvage The Promise for Abram: *"I want you to take Hagar, my Egyptian servant, as another wife."* Now living with the consequences of my contrived compromise, I could hardly believe I had spoken such words to my husband.

Playing God always costs more than you ever can foresee. Regardless how foolproof your plan appears, if it opposes or seeks to circumvent God's sovereignty, rest assured there is pain waiting just beyond where your vision fails. Even if in all your worldly wisdom you assess the possible damages and decide the consequences are worth playing God in your life, the cost of the counterfeit you create will exceed what you predict every time.

I compromised my marriage and gave my beloved Abram to another woman because I did not trust The God to fulfill His word. I gave away my enviable position as Abram's only wife because I thought I had a better plan. In doing so, I lost my dignity and the respect of others, and diminished my position of authority.

The initial cost of my compromise was damage to my household. Once clear lines of good order and stability were blurred, disorder and confusion became my new normal. The impending cost of my compromise was the quickly approaching and inescapable counterfeit promise embodied in Hagar's unborn child, igniting my vicious jealousy and Hagar's intolerable pride. I would not realize the ultimate cost of my compromise for many years.

Chaos was looming not only in our tent but also among all our people because I'd forgotten who I was. Abram had to remind me I was still in charge, but even with his prompting, I didn't manage as I had before, with wisdom, strength, and dignity. I ruled with malice and spite, the natural offspring of jealousy and bitterness.

Abram told me to deal with Hagar as seemed right to me. Regrettably for Hagar, unbridled anger and brutality seemed right to a hopeless, faithless, dead woman walking. I treated Hagar so harshly that she fled into the wilderness to escape my wrath, doubtless believing she stood a better chance of survival alone in the desert than under my sadistic hand. She may have been right.

SHATTERED
Happily, I had not seen Hagar for a few days when Abram came to our tent in the middle of the afternoon,

hysterical with the news of her disappearance. For one second I almost scoffed—until the sickening reality of the reason for his anguish became apparent. It wasn't only Hagar who was lost; it was Abram's child, the only child he'd ever fathered.

Standing in our tent, he wept inconsolably as I began to envision her lifeless body lying at the bottom of a ravine in the hills to the east or shriveling in the scorching heat of the desert to the west. Having given up his search for Hagar, Abram had doubtless formed the same conclusion when no trace of her surfaced.

Now what had I done?

A vision of me so many years ago in Pharaoh's harem flashed into my mind, that exact, terrifying moment when I realized our attempts at self-provision and self-protection had doomed us to a life of agony and shame. This time, I had ruined everything. This time, there was no Pharaoh to offer a pardon from my scheme. This time, the cost would be tallied in lost and ruined lives. Hagar and her child were gone forever, probably already dead somewhere in the wilderness that stretched thousands of miles around us. My husband was shattered.

MANY MILES TO GO

If my journey ended here—watching my husband reap the cruel harvest of my compromise—you could rightly say I got what I deserved. What I deserved was living the rest of my life in the wretchedness of realizing the price of playing God:

> My place of honor at Abram's side was gone, forfeited when my need to take control convinced me I should share my husband with my handmaiden. With brazen self-will I'd rent the fabric of our marriage. Now I was staring into the dark faces of Loneliness and Regret, destined to be my new lifelong companions.

> Ten years of our lives were gone, blown like sand across the endless desert into nothingness because I grew weary of waiting for The God; because I could not endure the pain of disappointment one more month and chose to travel a counterfeit path toward our destination.

> The Promise we'd chased so long and so far was gone, annulled by my raging jealousy that sent Abram's child to its death in the desert. Abram and I would spend the remainder of our lives in futility and bitterness, waiting to die childless in the ever-increasing desolation of our desert.

> My dignity was gone, eaten alive by my rage. Where once I'd walked in the light of authority and honor, I would now skulk in the shadows, hoping to avoid looks of contempt I knew I deserved.

Those things should have served as the landmarks for the final miles of my life's voyage—had I been the Navigator. Gratefully, there were many miles and many twists and turns still ahead of me. My journey doesn't end in wretchedness because despite my dead faith, my compromising, my cruelty, the counterfeit I'd created, even playing God, the Promise Maker never faltered.

As I stood helplessly watching Abram weep, my remorse so heavy I could barely breathe, I knew there was no way to undo all I'd done. I could no more retrace all the missteps made along this expedition and choose a different way than I could go back and find my footprints in the ocean of ever-shifting sand we'd crossed. Only kindness I could never deserve could heal the mortal wounds I'd inflicted.

THE GOD WHO KNOWS YOUR NAME

Hagar came back. Inexplicably, unexpectedly, unharmed, and (most surprisingly) humble, she came back. As miraculous as her return was, what followed incredibly on her footsteps was something I'd judged lost forever under several tons of sand.

The days between Hagar's departure and her return were the darkest I can recall as Abram mourned the loss of his child and I mourned the loss of Abram. Though I'd neither seen nor heard any condemnation from him, I was sure he blamed me for the tragic loss of his child. Rightly so. I'd sent Hagar into the wilderness as surely as I'd sent Abram to her tent.

When Hagar came back, she brought Abram a message so miraculous it brought him to his knees:

> *Two days had passed since I'd watched Abram collapse in grief on the floor of our tent. On the third day, we heard a loud disturbance outside.*
>
> *It was nearly midday, but neither Abram nor I*

had stirred. He was lying on his mat with his back to me. I could hear him breathing and moving; I knew he was awake, but neither of us spoke.

We lay back to back in the hot, semi-shadow of the tent, alone together with our personal sorrows. It had been like this since that day. We would emerge from our tent well after sunrise, go through the tasks necessary to maintain some semblance of order in our household, and then retreat to our unspoken heartache.

The commotion outside became almost riotous and was moving closer. Its fervor began to frighten me. It must have frightened Abram, also, as he sat up and stared at our tent flap, as if expecting someone or something to barge through. Then suddenly silence. Or almost silence. I could still hear murmuring right outside our tent and then a small voice.

"May I enter?"

We were both sitting up now, jolted by the familiarity of the voice. I realized I wasn't breathing. I exhaled and looked at Abram who was looking at me.

"May I enter, please?" it asked again.

Abram shot up off his mat and was at the tent door in one step. Reaching for the tent flap, his hand stopped short. He took a deep breath.

"Who's there?" he asked haltingly.

"It's Hagar, Sarai's maid."

Abram's arm flung the tent flap back so hard it fell off its cording. There she was, kneeling outside our tent door, face turned toward the ground.

I was up now and at the door. I shook my head and squinted as the late morning sun temporarily blinded me. I couldn't focus on her face. Was I dreaming? Was I going to awake to find my husband's back still to me, his child still gone? [Please, no more nightmares!]

But I wasn't dreaming. She was there. By the time my eyes adjusted and I could see her clearly, Abram had taken her hand and helped her stand. He was gazing at her, at her still round stomach, in disbelief. He placed his hands on her shoulders and smiled at her, then turned to me. In an instant, he swept me off the ground.

"They're back, Sarai! Hagar and our child are back!"

He was laughing and weeping as he held me in his arms. After a moment, he set me back on the ground. When we turned to Hagar, still standing at the door of our tent, eyes still downcast, she was crying as well.

[Was this the same haughty young woman I had terrorized with my cruelty? Where were her smirk and her prideful eyes?]

Abram went to her and lifted her head with his hand. "Hagar, why are you crying? Can't you see how happy I am that you've come back?"

"My tears are for my mistress, Sarai."

[For me? What?]

"My tears are tears of shame for how I behaved toward you, Mistress. I've come to submit myself to your authority. The Messenger said I must."

I was dumbfounded. Abram was not.

"What messenger, Hagar? Someone told you to come back?"

"My lord, a Messenger of The God Who Sees [35] found me by a spring in the wilderness. He knew me and called me by name. He said, 'Hagar, Sarai's

maid, where have you come from and where are you going?' When I told him I had fled Sarai, he said 'Return to your mistress, and submit yourself to her authority.'[36] *Here I am."*

With those last three words, she looked directly at me. I braced myself for a sneer that she'd hope Abram wouldn't notice. I was taken aback by the complete sincerity I saw.

She turned to Abram. "My lord, if I may, there's more; not about Sarai, about your child."

"What? Yes! Go on!"

"The Messenger said, 'Behold, you are with child, and you will bear a son and you will call him Ishmael, because God has heard you.'"[37]

Abram fell to his knees. Now he was the one dumbfounded. After a few seconds, he looked up at me.

"Ishmael." *He smiled as he repeated the name to me.* "A son, Sarai! An heir from my body, just as God promised, and his name is Ishmael."

GET THE PARTY STARTED!

Straight away, Abram sent runners throughout our people with a message that Hagar and his child lived and the night would be one of celebration. All work was to stop immediately and neighbors were to gather for a celebratory meal. There was so much to do. I hurriedly made my way to the tent of our household servants to instruct them.

I passed Hagar on my way. She was already in the food preparation tent, filling table urns with water. Our eyes met as I passed, but again there was no look of scorn only a modest smile before she turned back to her work. The change in her baffled me. It also left me ashamed for how cruelly I'd treated her.

I found several servants and told them to make the tables ready. We'd need an abundance of food for the feast Abram intended, so I tasked some of the older women with making more bread, grinding herbs, and filling many bowls with oil. I sent others to help Hagar with the water urns and to draw more from the wells. Several of the men had already headed to the herd with Eliezer to select the fattest goats for slaughter.

My work completed, I headed back to dress for the evening's festivities. Entering our tent, alone with Abram for the first time since Hagar's return, a shroud of cold fear wrapped around me. What if Abram's jubilance at Hagar's return was only a temporary reprieve from the pain I'd caused? What if the despair he'd fallen into was born of justifiable anger toward me greater than his capacity to forgive? What if the warmth I'd always seen in his soft brown eyes had turned to cold indifference? What if I got what I deserved?

"What are you wearing tonight?" I asked as nonchalantly as possible once inside.

"I don't know. Pick something you like and I'll wear that."

"Oh. Okay." [Something I liked. He wanted to wear something I liked. Could it be?]

I rummaged through his robes. "Here. This blue always looks good on you." I handed him one of the robes we'd acquired so long ago in Egypt. He looked at me and smiled. There was nothing behind his smile but the good, faithful man I'd always known. Of all the things I'd seen this day, Abram's faithful smile was the most amazing.

I turned and began browsing through my jewelry chest. I'd had neither a reason nor desire to dress festively for so long, I felt I was seeing the beauty of the glittering stones and polished metals for the first time. Abram must have been watching me stare in wonder at the dazzling box.

"Sarai, wear that gold necklace with the green jasper beads I bought from that caravan in Haran. You know the one?"

"With the really big beads and the gold leaves? That one?"

"Yes. I love that on you. It brings out your eyes."

I heard the flirtation in his voice and something inside me quivered. [My heart?] I would never understand Abram's love for me. Even now, after 60 years of marriage and all we'd just been through (more precisely, after all the pain I'd recently caused), he still spoke to me as a suitor. How had I let my heart wander so far from this good man? How long had it been since I returned his flirtations? I couldn't remember.

I turned to look at him. "Of course. I like that one, too." He smiled more broadly and continued dressing.

I remembered the day he bought that piece. Even then, he told me he chose it because the green reminded him of my eyes. Sumerian jewelry was famous for being, shall I say, ostentatious, but the beads on that necklace were large even for my taste.

In truth, that necklace had never been among my favorites, though I would never have said so to Abram. I had others I'd prefer to wear this night—some of my lapis lazuli to match Abram's robe, perhaps—but I would wear those gaudy green beads every day for the rest of my life if Abram asked.

That night musicians played, Abram danced, and I watched in bewilderment. Soon the echo of questions I asked more than a decade earlier began to drown out the lyres, bells, and drums: How was any of this possible? This was not the way of the world.

People don't simply reappear after being lost in the desert; they stay lost and are assumed dead.

Prideful people don't decide one day to kneel at your tent door and weep in repentance; they stay prideful.

Shattered men who've lost the desire to rise in the morning don't dance in the evening; they stay shattered.

Bitter women trapped in the nightmare of regret for playing God don't awaken to find they've been freed from the consequences; they stay trapped.

Beneath the clamor of these questions and musings, three words Hagar spoke earlier began to whisper and then roar in my mind. Of all the impossibilities that had recently become realities, Hagar's words as she reported her time away from our caravan were the most astonishing.

It wasn't that The God's messenger told Hagar she

would have a son or that The God personally picked a name for the child. It wasn't that He found her in the vast desert and told her to return to us. It wasn't even her genuine humility or changed countenance. What kept playing and replaying in my thoughts was that The God's messenger called her "Hagar, ***Sarai's*** maid."

He didn't call her "Hagar, Abram's wife" or "Hagar, the mother of Abram's child." He called her "Sarai's maid."

Sarai's maid.

Sarai's maid.

I realized I wasn't breathing as I repeated the phrase over and over in my thoughts then gasped as I realized the reason these words astonished me so: The God knew my name.

What manner of God would know *my* name? This is Abram's adventure.

Isn't it?

I had never prayed to this God, had never seen this God, had never heard this God. How could He know me, Sarai the Contentious, Sarai the Barren, most recently Sarai the Cruel Control Freak?

Could He see me? Could He hear me? Where was He?

He speaks to Abram, He spoke to Hagar, and now He's calling *me* by name?

Who is this God?

This God did not have so much as an idol of wood to offer prayers and petitions, and yet He spoke. This God did not have a temple for offering sacrifices, and yet He walked a covenant. This God did not even have a name, and yet He knew *mine*.

The God identified Hagar as *my* maid, her place in the story was in *my* care, under *my* authority. With those three words, "Hagar, Sarai's maid," I was repositioned. I still had a part in The Promise narrative.

Something in my heart softened as I realized I was seen.

I mattered.

THIS GOD OF MORE

Abram was right. This God was not like the gods we feared or strived to please in Sumer. He wasn't an idol made by the hands of our father, demanding constant praise and prayer but never speaking. He spoke freely to both master and servant. He didn't reside in a massive temple attended day and night by priests and scribes. He lived in the sky and in the desert and on the mountain. He lived in the morning haze, the blazing noon, and the darkest night. He didn't demand fearful service. He inspired whole-hearted worship.

He was more than the moon and the sun and the stars I'd worshipped. He was more than the wealth, power, and control I'd sought. He was more than my eyes could see, my ears could hear, or my mind could conceive, although I still didn't know how much more. He was mysterious, yet not fearsome; invisible, yet not hidden.

As I reflected on this God of more and mystery, my recently returned heart began to swell, first with gratitude, then with hope. I was grateful Hagar and her son had not perished in the wilderness. I was grateful Abram's eyes were still brown and warm and honest. I was grateful I'd not gotten what I deserved. Gratitude for what has been or what is begets hope for what will be.

Hope flooded my heart, drowning the jealousy that just days before threatened to engulf me. My new hope was not in the expectation of what I might gain from this adventure, not even in the approaching birth of the son Abram would finally have. It was hope in this God of power who spoke to the mighty and the humble, who sent a servant back to her ignoble mistress, a son back to his mourning father, and a husband back to his heartbroken wife. My hope was in The God who knew my name.

HOPE IN HIS FAITHFULNESS
The faithfulness of The God is the source of hope.

You have the advantage of your place in the timeline of history to read about The God's faithfulness in your Bible. Four thousand years ago, none of His stories—including mine—had been recorded. I wasn't learning of The God from the pages of a book. I was learning of Him experientially, moment by moment, breath by breath.

The God who knew my name knows yours: "I have summoned you by name; you are mine" (Isaiah 43:1 NIV). Not only does He know your name, your Bible says He knows everything about you. Everything. The good, the not so good, the really, *really* not good. Yes, even that. Yet, He never turns away: "The Lord Himself goes before you and will be with you; He will never leave you nor forsake you" (Deuteronomy 31:8 NIV).

In fact, He is so captivated by you, He has carved your name on the palms of His hands: "See, I have engraved you on the palms of My hands" (Isaiah 49:16 NIV). You make Him so happy, He sings about you: "He will take delight in you with gladness...He will rejoice over you with joyful songs" (Zephaniah 3:17 NLT). And His devotion to you is so complete, He vows to never leave you: "Surely I am with you always, even to the very end of the age" (Matthew 28:20 NIV).

God's kindness eternally protects you, His sovereignty perpetually provides a way for you, and His faithfulness relentlessly pursues you. There is hope in the faithfulness of God, about whom your Bible says, "God is no mere human! He doesn't tell lies or change his mind. **God always keeps his promises!**" (Numbers 21:19 CEB).

I was 76 years old when Ishmael was born. I believed I'd seen the fulfillment of The Promise to Abram and that my dream of a child would remain a dream. Our tent would finally house a child, but that child would not be mine, and I supposed I could find peace in that. I was content to finish my journey as Abram's childless wife, but "content" doesn't describe how my adventure ended any more than "wretched." (Look how many pages you have left to read!) My story wasn't over; it really had just begun.

WHEN GOD BREATHES

The anguish of Hagar's disappearance awakened a fierce paternal protectiveness in Abram. To insure we'd not face that particular horror again, Abram moved Hagar into our tent immediately after she returned. Having no children of my own, I assumed after Ishmael was born, Abram would allow Hagar and the baby to move back to her tent. I credit my inexperience as a parent for that bit of wishful thinking.

Abram's fatherly nature only intensified after Ishmael's birth. Separating Hagar from her newborn son was out of the question (I was in agreement with that), so sharing my home with another woman and a baby became my permanent new reality. The cost of my compromise continued to accrue in ways I had never foreseen. I shared my husband with Hagar for one night; now it seemed I might share my home with her forever.

You're probably wondering how Hagar and I were able to abide such close quarters, considering our history. All I can tell you is she was so different after her encounter with The God that while I won't go so far as to say we were friends, we weren't enemies. She was attentive to

Ishmael and never again disrespectful of Abram or me. We hung woven goat hair curtains to divide our large tent into three sections and insure a degree of privacy for everyone. It wasn't ideal, but we managed—more or less.

Time passed. We all adjusted, though not without some friction. My contentment as I watched Abram with Ishmael allowed me to regain my self-control, and therefore my dignity. I never again allowed my temper to run roughshod over those around me, but I was who I had always been and would always be, Sarai the Contentious.

ISHMAEL

From the beginning, Ishmael was a beautiful child. I saw Abram in his strong brow, distinct profile, the set of his jaw, but when he reached for me, as he often did, his eyes were Hagar's, piercing black. More than just beautiful, he was smart and fierce, learning early how to assert his will. Still assuming Ishmael was the fulfillment of The Promise, I thought both would be important for his future as the leader of our people in Canaan and beyond.

Abram was a good father. Did I even have to say it? By the time Ishmael was eight years old, he accompanied Abram almost everywhere he went. They quickly became inseparable. I'd never seen a father love a son more.

Abram never tired of teaching Ishmael about our people, about Terah and Haran and the family we left behind to follow The Voice of The God. Abram taught him about shepherding our flocks, the heartbeat of our business: breeding, land management, the best pasture grasses, and finding good water. He even took Ishmael into business dealings so he could observe how to barter deals skillfully to increase blessing for the day he would take over our family's business.

As Ishmael grew, Abram taught him about The God, telling him again and again the stories of chasing The Promise across the desert in search of our new home. Abram told how The God appeared to him at Shechem, and then they journeyed together to visit the altar he built there. Abram described in detail the covenant in the desert where The God promised to protect him and bless his descendants for all time, even though Abram slept through the most important parts of the process.

Ishmael wasn't the only one hearing the stories. Abram told the stories to the men as he walked with them or worked side by side with them. The men told the stories to their families and neighbors. The Mighty God of Abram soon became famous in settlements all over the land.

WHO ARE YOU TALKING TO?
One afternoon just after I turned 90, I was sitting in the shade of the large oak trees near our tent when I saw

Abram approaching. Ishmael, who was 13 at the time, had left with him that morning but now Abram was alone. It was past time for our midday meal, so I assumed Ishmael, who seemed perpetually hungry, stopped along the way to eat at the home of one of our friends.

Abram had been out all morning. He looked tired. He'd want something to eat. I got up and headed to our tent and began laying out some meat and bread left from my meal. My back was to the door when Abram entered and spoke two of the most mystifying words I'd ever heard.

"Hello, Sarah."

It was Abram's voice, but who was he talking to? I turned to look at him, standing in the doorway. The sun behind him made me squint, but I could see well enough to know there was no one else in the tent. He said it again.

"Hello, Sarah."

[A new nickname? Princess? I'm 90 years old and suddenly I'm his 'Princess'? Oh, no! At 99, had age finally caught up with my Abram? Was his mind slipping?]

I was about to correct him with 'Contentious' when he took a few steps toward me and my breath caught. It had been more than 13 years since I'd seen that look on Abram's face. It could have been 300 and I would have recognized it. This wasn't age taking hold of my husband's mind. This was time spent with The God.

"Oh, no," I said, aloud this time. [Something was about to change. Something big. Something always changed when The God spoke to Abram.] "You've been with Him again."

Abram smiled. "Yes. I've been with El Shaddai."

"Who?"

"El Shaddai, Sarah. His name is El Shaddai."

"Whose name is El Shaddai? I meant you've been with The God. And why do you keep calling me 'Princess'?" [Abram was visibly wound up about something and spouting off names I'd never heard. I was confused and a tad annoyed.]

"God's name is El Shaddai. God, Who led us out of Haran, Who delivered us from Egypt, Who gave Ishmael, He has a name, Sarah. His name is El Shaddai."

[The God has a name? The God has a name. The God has a name! I'm reasonably sure my mouth

dropped open as I stared at Abram. I repeated the name to myself a few times, then tried it aloud].

"El Shaddai?" I spoke slowly, intentionally emphasizing the three syllables of this strange, new name that in my language means 'God Who is Enough'.

"Yes! El Shaddai!"

"The God's name is El Shaddai?"

*"Yes—well, no. I mean, yes, that's His name, but no, He's not **the** God, He's just God."*

*I hesitated before asking, "Is He 'Just God' or is He 'El Shaddai'? I'm not following." [Maybe it was age catching up with **me**. I was 90, after all.]*

Abram took a deep breath and spoke more slowly, as he did when he explained things to Ishmael for the first time, and surprisingly, I wasn't offended. The God having a name was shocking, and I was genuinely confused and wanted to understand. In one breath, Abram was telling me The God was 'Enough,' in the next breath He was 'Just God,' and to really mix things up, he kept calling me 'Princess.'

"Once more, please, and slowly."

*"God's name is El Shaddai, but He's not **the** God, Sarah. He is God, the only God. Those thousands of 'gods' we worshipped back in Sumer, they're not real; their names are as meaningless as our worship of them was. There is only One, there has always only been One, and the One we've been following is He."*

He paused, no doubt waiting for a rebuttal from me. I said nothing. A few slow blinks from me filled the silence, so he went on.

"God is El Shaddai. El Shaddai is God. There is no other God because El Shaddai is Enough. He is God of everything that ever has been or ever will be. He is El Shaddai, God Sovereign."

In those few sentences, my entire life's belief system began to collapse. In my mind, every idol I'd ever bowed to crumbled into a heap of ash or rust. I stood silent and motionless, as the words sank in.

He went on:

"There's more—much more—and it's about you, but I'm pretty sure that conversation is going to take some time, and right now, I have something else He told me to do first. I came to let you know Ishmael and I may be gone for a day or two, but

don't worry; we're fine—or at least we will be. I'll tell you the rest in a few days."

He turned to leave.

"Wait! Can you at least tell me why you keep calling me 'Princess'?"

He turned back and took a few steps closer to me. "El Shaddai gave you a new name. He said your name is no longer Sarai. Your name from this moment will be Sarah. You are His Princess. And mine. Forever."[38]

Me, mute and motionless again.

"And He changed my name, too. He calls me Abraham, not Abram."[39]

He smiled at me as he exaggerated the "hhh" sound in each of our new names. He was standing close to me and I could feel his warm breath fall on my face as he did so. After a few seconds, I smiled back.

"Okay, Abraham," I said his name for the first time, mimicking his exaggerated "hhh" sound. I liked the softness the added letter lent his name. I said it again: "Abraham." He liked it, too, from the look on his face.

> *"I'll be back as soon as I can, Sarah," he said, as easily as if he'd called me 'Princess' all our lives. Then he was gone. He hadn't even eaten.*

I stood alone in our same old tent, but I was living in a brand-new world: a world of one God Who is Enough; a world where I am not the contentious wife of Abram, I'm the Princess of Abra*ham*. I knew when I saw the look on Abraham's face something was about to change. I suspected maybe another move, but never thought there would be new names and a world ruled by one Sovereign God.

Truthfully, Abraham's statements about the gods of Sumer not being "real" were easier to accept than you might think. In 90 years, I'd never seen any proof they were more than dead wood or cold metal. I took Abraham's words more as confirmation of my suspicions than sacrilege. Still, one God of everything would take some getting used to.

Everything meant every person. It meant me. El Shaddai was God of Sarah. El Shaddai was Sovereign over Sarah. El Shaddai was Enough for Sarah.

THE BEAUTIFUL NAME
I repeated the name to myself several times. El Shaddai. El Shaddai. God Who is Enough. Enough. He is Enough.

Suddenly, I understood.

At last, I understood.

After almost 25 years, I understood.

More than two decades worth of questions were answered in His name. He is God and He is Enough. Enough to provide and protect. Enough to deliver us from Egypt. Enough to save Hagar. Enough to give Abram a son. And Enough to know the name of a dejected, empty, broken water urn and fill her with hope in her old age. Every impossibility I'd pondered since leaving Haran was possible because He was Enough.

I said the name aloud: "El Shaddai." It was a beautiful name. I said it again: "El Shaddai!" I wanted to shout the beautiful new name—no, I wanted to sing it. I wanted one of the musicians to write a song whose only words were "El Shaddai, El Shaddai, El Shaddai!" so everyone could sing it with me.

He was El Shaddai. He was God. He was Enough—and He called me *Princess*. El Shaddai, Whose name I now knew, gave me more than a new name. It was a new beginning! At 90 years old, I was starting over!

"HHHHEY"

The difference between Sarai and Sarah is one letter, but that one specific letter completely transformed me. The Hebrew letter El Shaddai added to my name (and to Abraham's) is the *hey,* which in my language makes the sound of your letter H, the sound of breath exhaled, as when Abraham exaggerated our names and breathed on my face.

In Hebrew, letters not only make sounds, they have meaning, sometimes many meanings. The letter *hey* represents the divine breath and the creative power of God and a picture of the presence of God within the human heart.[40] More astounding—if it's possible—than those meanings is that the letter *hey* represents the grace and goodness of God poured out [breathed into!] His works.[41] El Shaddai breathed all this into Abraham and me as part of the revelation of who He said we were, our revealed identities.

Can you begin to glimpse the beauty of my name? El Shaddai wasn't just calling me Princess, as glorious as that was. He was putting new life in me, **His** life. He breathed my name and called His presence and His essence to manifest in my heart. The underlying truth that you may never have heard before is that Sarah wasn't a *new* name from El Shaddai. Sarah is who El Shaddai always knew I was. His breath revived the Princess He created within me from the beginning of time. It revealed to the world the strong, gracious woman He'd seen all along.

God breathed and Sarai transformed into Sarah. The old identity of "Barren" I'd branded across my heart so many years ago cracked, the hardened scars giving way to soft flesh. More than fifteen hundred years later, the Prophet Ezekiel's words in your Bible would describe exactly what happened when El Shaddai breathed on me: "I will give you a new heart and put a new spirit in you; I will remove your heart of stone and give you a heart of flesh."[42] My new heart was quiet, not quarrelsome; gentle, not belligerent; confident, not contentious.

El Shaddai had seen me with one breath. And He had seen me despite my empty womb. He reframed my nature even though I was "flawed" as my culture viewed women. I was still part of the story, even at 90 years old, and that revelation brought a resurrection of hope and peace deep in my soul. God spoke my name and His breath anointed my secret place of heartbreak. My shoulders drew back, my jaw unclenched, my fists opened, and my face relaxed.

When God changes you—and only He can truly change you—you are changed forever. His Spirit joins with your identity and you are literally a new person. Your Bible says when that happens you lay aside your old self like yesterday's robes and "put on the new self, created after the likeness of God." [43]

In one breath, Sarai the Contentious became Sarah the Gracious, and the shroud of fear, manipulation, and insecurity born from a lifetime of the pain of disappointment behind which I'd hidden transformed into a mantle of dignity, honor, and authority. I may have been wearing the same robe and veil as a moment earlier, but my heart was dressed in splendor such as I'd never known.

NEVER OUT OF STYLE

All my life people called me "beautiful." Beautiful and broken. My near obsession with clothes and jewelry, almost as legendary as my beauty, was a cover-up: keep the attention on the outside and maybe, just maybe, no one will notice the wounded, fearful spirit just below the surface. My old name was proof of how well that worked.

True beauty, the kind that lasts and that is worth more than the fortune I had spent on fine fashion and elaborate jewelry, comes from within, when your spirit is made gentle and quiet—uncontentious—by the Breath of God. Thousands of years later one of the disciples, who walked with my Greatest Grandson, would write about the transformation that occurred in my heart when the Spirit of El Shaddai changed my name:

> *"Your beauty should not come from outward adornment, such as elaborate hairstyles and the wearing of gold jewelry or fine clothes. Rather, it should be that of your inner self, the unfading beauty of a gentle and quiet spirit, which is of great worth in God's sight. For this is the way the holy women of the past who put their hope in God used to adorn themselves. They submitted*

themselves to their own husbands, like Sarah, who obeyed Abraham and called him her lord. You are her daughters if you do what is right and do not give way to fear" (1 Peter 3–6 NIV).

By now you know a "gentle and quiet spirit" was not part of Sarai's wardrobe. My greatest grandson's disciple, Peter, could not have used me as an example in his fashion tip had not God totally changed me at my core. Only God could change my heart. Only God can change yours, but once He breathes on you and His Spirit changes your "name," the change is eternal.

It's a transformation that clothes "your inner self" in gentleness as you relinquish control and place your life wholly in the care of God Who is Enough. Knowing He has mapped every step of your journey, you can walk even the most obscure path in quiet confidence. Regardless how many thousands of years separate you and me, some things never go out of style.

That disciple, Peter, the fisherman-turned-preacher, ended his fashion advice with, "You are [Sarah's] daughters if you do what is right and do not give way to fear." Doing what is right and not giving way to fear are not separate instructions. Doing what is right is living by faith rather than hiding in fear. Until the moment God breathed on me, fear ruled my life: fear of never being "enough," fear of failure, fear of disappointment, fear of not being in control, fear of losing my position, of being dishonored, disregarded, and disgraced. I'm sure you can understand at least one of those and can possibly add to that list.

I concealed my fear under "gold jewelry and fine clothes." I built a wall of contention to keep others from getting close enough to see my insecurities. I obsessed over the "how" of my life, forever trapped in an exhausting and futile struggle to turn the path where I thought it should lead. El Shaddai breathed peace; fear evaporated like morning dew on the desert sand.

RECEIVE THE HOLY SPIRIT

In your Bible, there's a story about another time God breathed a world-changing breath, not on two aged nomads in the desert but on a group of people hiding out in an upper room in the city of Jerusalem. In this story, Jesus appears to a group of His followers a few days after His crucifixion. The men and women are cowering in fear behind a locked door, until Jesus appears and breathes on them.

> *"On the evening of that first day of the week, when the disciples were together, with the doors locked for fear of the Jewish leaders, Jesus came and stood among them and said, 'Peace be with you!' After He said this, He showed them His hands and side. The disciples were overjoyed when they saw the Lord. Again Jesus said, 'Peace be with you! As the Father has sent me, I am sending*

you.' And with that He breathed on them and said, 'Receive the Holy Spirit'" (John 20:19–22).

God breathed on that group of frightened disciples and transformed them into some of the most courageous men and women of eternity. The word translated "breathed" here is the Hebrew *ruach* and is the word for "breath of God."[44]

The word *ruach* appears throughout your Bible as "wind" "breath," or "spirit". It's the almighty Wind that wipes out evil: *"The wicked are not so but they are like chaff which the wind [ruach] drives away"*. It's the fierce Breath that lays waste the wicked: *"He will strike the earth with the rod of His mouth, and with the breath [ruach] of His lips He will slay the wicked"*. It's the creative Spirit that moved over the dark, formless waters of the earth on the First Day of Creation, transforming darkness into glorious Light: *"The earth was formless and void, and darkness was over the surface of the deep, and the Spirit [ruach] of God was moving over the surface of the waters.* Wherever His breath goes—His divine, creative breath—everything changes.

In that upper room, Jesus breathed that powerful breath on His disciples, blowing their fear away like chaff and empowering them to forgive and move forward. This little band literally changed the world for all time by spreading Jesus' message of life, hope, and the power of resurrection. And it all started when He breathed on and into them.

Changing me from a contrary old woman desperate to cover my fear and shame in fine clothes and fancy jewelry into a gracious princess with a heart adorned in gentleness, peace, and joy may not read with the same element of drama as emboldening that quaking band of brothers and sisters, but the far-reaching effects were just as world-altering. I realized sometime later that all my years in the desert were El Shaddai's way of working out the fear-driven Sarai so He could speak the Sarah into me and then draw her out for the rest of the world. Contention doesn't nurture life. Princesses are blessed to be fruitful and multiply. I didn't know it yet, but the world needed a Princess.

I accepted my identity from God Who is Enough and thought that was enough. It was only the beginning.

WHY I LAUGHED

Abraham was gone two days. He returned late in the evening, exhausted, a bit bedraggled, but somehow more regal than I'd ever seen him. I'd awaited his return with cheerful expectation. He'd said there was more to tell me, "much more" than knowing God's name and becoming His Princess. Try as I might, I could not conceive anything more incredible.

I'd spent the two days Abraham was gone contemplating in amazement all the ways El Shaddai had proven Himself to be Enough all these years and reveling in the beauty of my name. Time spent meditating on God's kindness and sovereignty transforms you. I literally was not the same woman Abraham left just two days ago.

I was Contentious, now I'm Princess. My heart, once lost in the wilderness, now found rest in God who led it home. Once enslaved to the fear of the pain of disappointment, now I served Sovereign God, who never fails. Once convinced I had to struggle and play God to provide for and protect myself, now I knew God was my shield. Once tormented by my belief that I would never be enough, now I had peace knowing God was.

El Shaddai, Who knew me and named me, Who saw me and changed me, had given me a place that no one could take from me. I didn't have to scrap and scrape for it. I had not earned it and did nothing to deserve it. I had done most everything wrong, and still, He covered me in kindness and filled me with Life.

When he returned, Abraham's fatigue was obvious; rather than bombard him with the arsenal of questions I'd prepared, I fed him, rolled out his bed mat, and sat quietly as he fell into a deep sleep. He slept until well past sunrise the next day. While he slept, I decided I could wait until Abraham thought the time was right to share the rest of his conversation with El Shaddai. Surprisingly, waiting was something I was becoming rather good at.

THREE VISITORS

When Abraham finally awoke, he moved slowly, as if in pain. He ate breakfast then went to sit at the door of our tent. After an hour or more, it looked as though he'd fallen asleep in the midday heat. I was watching him, calmed by the steady rhythm of his breathing, when suddenly he raised his head, jumped to his feet, and dashed out of the tent, straightening his robes about himself as he flew. Startled, I stepped over to the door to see where he was going. *What in the world?!?* As soon as my eyes adjusted to the sunlight, I saw he was running to meet Three Men who'd approached out of nowhere. I stepped back into the shadow of the tent where I could better observe without being observed.

The Three were strangers, yet there was a familiarity about Them that immediately put me at ease. As I watched, Abraham bowed himself to the earth in front of The Three. [45] Who were these Visitors before Whom Abraham prostrated Himself and why did I feel I knew Them when I certainly had never seen Them before? I could tell Abraham was speaking to Them, but couldn't hear the conversation. Suddenly, Abraham was on his feet, running toward our tent. Pain or no pain, he was moving swiftly.

"Sarah, quickly! Prepare some bread cakes!"

"I can make bread cakes, but not quickly. Who are these Visitors? Are they staying for dinner?"

"Very special Guests, Sarah, and yes, they are staying."

"Okay. Then maybe after eating you can tell me about the rest of your conversation with El Shaddai?"

That slowed him down long enough to take my hands in his and step closely to me.

He looked deeply at me with a young man's twinkle. [Oh, my husband! I may have actually blushed!]. "These Guests are part of what I still have to tell you, but first, bread cakes!"

With that, he smiled, dropped my hands, and scampered away. (Yes, I said 'scampered'). As he left the tent he threw "I'm going to go get milk and prepare a calf" over his shoulder like he was tossing a barley bag onto a cart. I chuckled lightly to myself at his exuberance, then headed to my flour bin.

Never had my hands moved so fast as I worked the barley flour into small loaves. My barley bread was still Abraham's favorite. I smiled at the memory of stopping mid-bake that hot afternoon in Haran when Abraham had come home to tell me we were moving. Then I sighed as I realized I would have to wait until our Guests left for Abraham to tell me the rest of his conversation with El Shaddai a few days ago.

Soon Abraham was back with milk, curds, and the calf he'd prepared for our Guests to eat. He smiled but didn't speak as he rushed into our tent to fetch the still-hot bread. Abraham joined the Three under the trees and began to serve Them the meal we'd prepared.

I was quietly out of sight in our tent, watching the Three eat the bread I'd baked, when I heard it. I can't tell you how but I knew with complete certainty what I heard was The Voice: **"Where is your wife Sarah?"** [46]

El Shaddai had spoken to Abraham, He'd said my name to Hagar, and even told Abraham He changed my name, but never had I heard His Voice. Still, my heart knew it at the first syllable. He might have been addressing Abraham, but He was speaking to me. I gasped.

"There, in the tent," Abraham answered. [47]

I hadn't yet exhaled when One of the Three began the most fateful conversation of my life. His words were clear and bold as if He were inside the tent standing in the shadows beside me:

"I will surely return to you at this time next year; and behold, Sarah your wife will have a son." [48]

In an instant, I understood the certainty I'd seen in Abraham's eyes long ago in Haran, the conviction I'd heard in His voice when he told me about the covenant, and the confidence I'd seen on his face when he came home two days ago to tell me El Shaddai called me Princess. Words so incredible, spoken by any other than the One Whose Voice I now heard, could have provoked doubt, skepticism, even derision. They did not. My heart heard The Voice and immediately believed His Promise.

The conversation I had with myself at hearing these words that your Bible documents was simply my mind trying to catch up to my heart: "A son? A child from my body and Abraham's? At our age, Abraham and I will share more than a bed mat as we lie down together? My dormant womb will revive and this all-but-dead body will conceive new life? [49] *I couldn't do this even when I was young. How exactly is this possible? Oh, I know: God is sitting under an oak tree eating bread with my husband, so of course, I am going to have a baby! Babies are the newest thing with the nonagenarian crowd!"*

Without warning, my heart laughed: "After I am worn out and my lord is old, will I now have this pleasure?" [50]

Abraham didn't hear my private thoughts or my heart's laughter so I'm sure God's next question confounded him: **"Why did Sarah laugh and say, 'Will I really have a child, now that I am old?' Is anything too hard for the Lord? I will return to you at the appointed time next year, and Sarah will have a son."** [51]

God and Abraham turned toward where I was

standing in the tent. I jumped back and covered my mouth in alarm. Did I just do that out loud? I thought I was just thinking a giggle. Oh, no! I hope I did not offend. Now what have I done?

Realizing El Shaddai could not only speak to my heart but also could hear its every thought—and laugh—frightened me. I reacted without thinking, in just a whisper behind the tent flap, I said, "I did not laugh."

I don't know Who I thought I was talking to. I was alone in the tent. There'd been no footsteps in my direction, no commotion of any kind. The tent flap had not moved, but suddenly that seemingly empty tent completely filled with the presence of the Almighty One, The Voice, El Shaddai, the One Who is Enough.

He spoke again. This time I not only heard His words, I felt them. They were strong yet soft, discerning yet tender, and I know I detected a smile: **"Yes, you did laugh."**[52]

Every step of our journey has led to this moment: Me, hiding behind my tent flap, my heart laughing because of The Promise of God, and then denying it. This was my moment, my personal audience with El Shaddai. ***This*** conversation was with me, directly, not through my husband. El Shaddai didn't speak about me, He spoke to me. Loose strings of seemingly unrelated moments suddenly wove themselves together in my mind: This adventure had been for **us**, Abraham and me. Abraham **and** me.

If The Promise had just been about Abraham having a son, well, he had one—Ishmael. Abraham had a son. But not with me. Yet. Somewhere in The Promise, in the new country, in the Covenant, in this Providential Picnic, there was a seat saved just for **me**.

I couldn't feel my face, I couldn't move my arms, I couldn't ignite any thoughts. All I could do was stand there and involuntarily chuckle. It was unthinkable: I was 90! It was unimaginable: I had been so awful about this Promise. It was inconceivable: no, wait! Conceivable is exactly what this was. Conceivable is what God does in your head and heart when you've reached the end of yourself. Conceivable is the essence of the Creator. Conceivable is what He was working into me, and my response was the most spontaneous explosion of joy I'd ever experienced. I laughed!

For thousands of years, that laugh has often been misinterpreted as mockery toward El Shaddai. The word used to describe my laugh is the Hebrew word transliterated *tsachaq*.[53] It can mean "delight" or "derision." I'm not completely surprised when I hear that many choose to believe the latter definition. After all, in 90 years I'd earned a reputation of belligerence that could lead those who don't know me as intimately as you do to that conclusion.

I also understand how those who've not heard my story in my own words could construe my response, "I did not laugh," as simply more of Sarai the Quarrelsome, impudently arguing with Almighty God. You know I wasn't Sarai anymore. The Spirit of God had become part of my identity. I responded as Sarah, Princess, gracious and strong, yet, oh, so human. I was afraid. I was in the presence of Sovereign God, and I did exactly what most do when He shows us the contents of our hearts, I tried to deny it.

OUT OF HIDING

If you remember only one moment of our long trip together, I pray it is the four words El Shaddai spoke to my heart, "Yes, you did laugh." His words tenderly uncovered me from my hiding place in the doorway. He pulled the tent flap back on my unfathomable thoughts, the ones too deep for even me to truly know, and He brought me to a perfect moment of both retrospection and introspection. Simultaneously, images of a past full of regret and a future fulfilled shuffled through my mind.

If you've ever read those four words in your Bible and heard God's voice as stern and scolding or petulant and peevish, listen more closely, hear the kindness in His voice as He reveals the contents of my heart. What I heard was, "Yes, Princess, you laughed! You laughed because your faith is coming to life and it feels good! You laughed because you thought all this was over for you! You laughed because what has been promised to you defies logic and reason and, yet, it's going to happen! You laughed because you believe!"

That laugh was half incomprehension and half irony—the blessed, sacred, delightful irony. It was the same laugh you would enjoy if you jumped off one of your tall buildings and floated instead of plummeting. It was the delight of experiencing the One who is Alive and created Life for us to enjoy.

God wants to put His Sovereign hand into the issue, the real issue that keeps you from experiencing the depth of His love and abundance of His life, so He asks you a question. You have the choice, then, to answer at all, and to answer honestly. The depth of the question draws out the truth of the situation, and in that one glorious moment, there is healing.

My many-greats grandmother Eve hid in the bushes of the Garden and tried to conceal herself behind fig leaves after eating from the Tree of Knowledge because she was experiencing something she'd never felt before—fear and shame. With one question, Elohim drew her out. All He said was "Where are you?" [54] When He asked a similar question of me, "Why did Sarah laugh?" I didn't step boldly out of the tent and admit my laughter. Still,

His immeasurable kindness continued to draw my heart out of hiding.

Everything El Shaddai does is kindness, even those things you have experienced—maybe are even now experiencing—that seem difficult and *un*kind are designed to draw *your* heart out of hiding. He wants you to step out of the shadows and follow where His kindness leads because it leads you to—HIM!

Two millennia after my famous conversation with El Shaddai, the Apostle Paul wrote to people in a place called Rome about the miraculous work of El Shaddai's kindness: "Or do you disregard the riches of His kindness, tolerance, and patience, not realizing that God's kindness leads you to repentance?"[55] Repentance! That mind-blowing moment when Light shines into darkness, Truth replaces error, and you choose a new path.

I'd spent decades mistakenly thinking of myself as an unnamed "also appeared" in the great unfolding drama of "Abraham and The Promise." At 90 years old, having no legacy except that of Abraham's barren wife, I believed when my life ended it would have been as pointless as the sand dunes I watched come and go all day. In a moment's time, they were blown away, not even one grain of sand left to attest they'd ever been there: Forgotten. Unimportant. Inconsequential. They…didn't…matter.

Even if The Promise proved true and Abraham's descendants indeed outnumbered the stars, no one would remember the name of Ishmael's *step*mother. Hagar, perhaps, but not Sarah. I believed emphatically that I would die somewhere in this desert and be buried in the sand, my name disappearing in the desert wind as surely as all memory of my life. No one would remember Sarah.

Ha! Not remember me?!? All of Eternity remembers *me*! My name has been and is remembered—even honored—by millions upon millions—wait, make that billions—throughout history. Why? Because the kindness of God led me to repent as He opened the eyes of my heart to the absurdly glorious happy Truth—and I laughed!

EYES OF YOUR HEART

El Shaddai spoke to my heart, "Yes, you did laugh," so I could see the truth of why I laughed. When He reveals the contents of your heart, it's never to rebuke you, punish you, or shame you. In His everlasting kindness, God opens the eyes of your heart so you can see Truth, because once you see Truth, you are able to conceive the life of Promise He's called you to.

That life begins with stepping out of the camouflage of the bushes or from behind the shadow of a tent flap (or wherever you try to hide from El Shaddai) and into the Light of His plan of repentance. God sees you and

He asks you a question that only your heart can hear and only your heart can answer. Whatever the question, you can trust Him with the answer. He asks only so He can draw you closer to Him, close enough that He can lavish His kindness on you.

The same Apostle Paul who wrote of El Shaddai's kindness also wrote a letter to a church in Ephesus, asking God to "Open the eyes of their hearts, and let the light of Your truth flood in. Shine Your light on the hope You are calling them to embrace. Reveal to them the glorious riches You are preparing as their inheritance."[56] Hope and an inheritance of glory are His Promises to you! They are the truth you see when His kindness opens the eyes of your heart and fills you with His Light.

Truth kindles hope, hope ignites faith, and faith pleases God. In fact, your Bible says without faith it's impossible to please Him.

> *"Without faith it is impossible to please God, because anyone who comes to Him must believe that He exists and that He rewards those who earnestly seek Him" (Hebrews 11:6, NIV).*

Please don't hear that as a warning that God is going to be angry with you when your faith falters. Everyone's faith falters along the journey. Everyone steps off the path and goes their own way at some point.

YOUR FAITH FUNNEL

God the Creator knows your shortcomings, weaknesses, and struggles. He knows hearts grow weary and become lost. He knows the path is sometimes hard to see and that sandstorms sometimes stop you from moving at all. He knows you are going to trip, stumble, and even fall at some point in life's wilderness.

Through all these, it's God's grace that makes a way in the wasteland, rescues your heart, steadies your footing, and then stands you up to walk again. Your Bible says "For it is by grace you have been saved through faith—and this is not from yourselves, it is the gift of God" (Ephesians 2:8, NIV). You aren't responsible for mustering up enough faith to please Him. You simply receive it from Him.

You and I are divided by centuries, by cultures, by language, by specific experiences, but El Shaddai's gift of faith is the same for us, just as it always has been and always will be for all people. In life, we all encounter "situations" that present us with a choice. It may be a "wilderness," a "harem," a "consequence," a "counterfeit," a dry desert, or a fertile valley. Whatever the situation, the choice we have is to allow it to shape and mold us—to transform us—to reveal the person God says we are, or to reject the opportunity for transformation and revelation because it is too hard and hurtful. It's a moment of exercising our beautiful free will to receive or reject a deeper revelation from and deeper relationship with our kind El Shaddai.

The early years of my life, I consistently rejected such opportunities and missed the exercise of my faith. What doesn't get exercised atrophies at best, dies at worst. As you know, by the time the three Guests arrived on our front porch, my faith, though recently revived by the breath of El Shaddai when He changed my identity, still was badly withered.

Until the kindness of El Shaddai opens the eyes of your heart, you can't see life's "situations" as opportunities. Once the eyes of your heart are open, you can see that what's happening around you is happening "for" you, not "to" you. When you begin to see situations as food and water for your faith, then your faith grows, expanding into a wide conduit of the grace and power of El Shaddai. Then El Shaddai, The God Who Is Enough, is pleased to generously lavish His Enough on you. It pleases Him so much, that if you lean in close, you may just hear Him laugh with delight.

Faith pleases God because faith is the funnel through which He pours His power and grace into your life. The bigger your faith is, exercised through experience, the more of His power and grace He gets to pour into you. The smaller your faith, the less grace and power you are able to contain.

This condition of having "no faith" or "little faith" displeases Him because He has so much to heap on you and you have no space to contain it. This is the reason my greatest grandson spent so much time teaching His disciples lessons of faith: not to point out that they were lacking, but to teach them how to have more.

Trudging through the desert, relying only on what you see to guide you, your faith funnel starts to constrict. After time, it can close completely, making your life as dry and fruitless as the desert around you. But following the Voice of God, seeing Truth with the eyes of your heart, your faith funnel opens wide. God gives His gift of faith without measure so He can pour grace and power into your life in abundance. There's nothing you need more and nothing that pleases Him more than your life overflowing with His saving grace.

LIFE FEELS GOOD!

I started this journey with a closed faith funnel, only trusting what I could see, could figure out, or could make happen for myself. Remember, I'd spent my life worshiping "gods" of wood and metal. It's no wonder I could not conceive. I was chasing a supernatural Promise depending on my natural abilities. I didn't know Who I was following and had never heard His voice. The moment my heart heard God declare I would bear Abraham's child, my faith funnel opened wide and His grace and power flooded every part of me with new life. Life felt good and I laughed!

> I laughed for joy as belief in The Promise of God overwhelmed me, reviving my dead dreams.

I laughed in amazement that my journey wasn't over, that the best paths were still ahead of me, waiting to be traveled.

I laughed with relief that the sovereignty of God was more than enough to set right the twists, turns, and missteps I'd made along the way.

I laughed in wonder that The Promise meant I would leave a flesh and blood legacy even after I left this world.

I laughed for pure delight as my once-dead faith exploded, filling my heart with hope.

THE BEGINNING OF RIGHTEOUSNESS

That beautiful laugh, so maligned for millennia, was the beginning of my righteousness. Your book of Romans says, "with the heart a person believes, resulting in righteousness." [57] My heart believed and roared with joy!

If you've ever struggled with the word "righteousness," be sure it has nothing to do with what you *do*. Righteousness is not a pattern of behavior; it is believing. The night of the covenant I discounted because Abraham slept through it, God said, "Your descendants will outnumber the stars," Abraham said, "I believe that," and God said, "You're righteous." [58]

God's declaration of Abraham's righteousness wasn't

a commentary on anything Abraham did or didn't do. Remember, Abraham slept through all the action that night. God called Abraham righteous because he *believed*. That's exactly what happened when I heard God say, "Sarah your wife will have a son": I believed. Yes, my thoughts bounced around like baby goats in spring, but I believed.

Once I believed, I was able to conceive. I'm not talking about conceiving a child—not yet. I'm talking about conceiving the truth of what God says. Up to that moment, I could not conceive that The Promise was for me. The idea that a woman as old as I could have a child simply could not take root and grow in my mind or my heart. Until I heard the words He spoke *to* me.

These words were not *about* me. I wasn't part of the conversation, part of the adventure, part of The Promise simply because I was Abraham's wife. I had a particular place at the table because El Shaddai wasn't just Abraham's God, He was my God, *our* God!

El Shaddai is your God, too (even if you don't yet know it), and your righteousness (like mine) is that when God's Word plants a seed of faith, you are able to let it take root, let it grow, and let the Life He's breathed into you come out of you. Sitting under the trees outside our tent, God spoke The Promise of a child to *me.* My mind heard the truth, my heart conceived the truth, and my body responded to the truth.

I laughed.

FOR ME!

As soon as I recovered my composure, my eyes looked out and found Abraham's face. He hadn't fainted in amazement as El Shaddai declared, "I will surely return to you at this time next year; and behold, Sarah your wife will have a son." Instead, he was looking at me with the same intensity he had as we sat on his favorite cushion in our house in Haran. For the first time, I realized what he was telling me that day so long ago: The Promise was not only for Abraham. The Promise was—had always been—for *me* too.

That was the "much more" Abraham was waiting to tell me. Two days earlier, God did more than reveal our names. He breathed new life into a decades old Promise and told Abraham something that caused him to laugh exactly as I did. That's right! I'm not making this up! Abraham laughed right out loud when God revealed the plan to him—that *we* would have a son together. He laughed, too, and the word in our Hebrew language for his laughter is the same word used a chapter later for mine.

> *"Then God said to Abraham, 'As for Sarai your wife, you shall not call her name Sarai, but Sarah shall be* her *name. I will bless her, and indeed I will give you a son by her. Then I will bless her, and she shall be a mother of nations; kings of peoples will come from her.' Then Abraham fell on*

his face and laughed [tsachaq], and said in his heart, 'Will a child be born to a man one hundred years old? And will Sarah, who is ninety years old, bear a child?'" (Genesis 17:15-17, NASB).

Abraham, whose unwavering belief in The Promise and in God earned him the title "righteous" many years earlier, fell down laughing when God said I would have a baby. Why wouldn't he? It's a hilarious idea that a man and woman as old as we could even get our bodies to cooperate with the necessary mechanics of making a baby.

To me, the truly astonishing parts of that echo of The Promise are the specific words God used: "I will give you a son by **her**." "I will bless **her**." "**She** shall be a **mother** of nations." "Kings of peoples will come from **her**." God wanted to remove all doubt for Abraham and for me: I was the one through whom El Shaddai would accomplish His Promise. Then, just to be sure there was no misinterpretation, He left heaven's throne to visit our tent so I could hear it directly from Him.

GROWING UP IN FAITH

I made an assertion when you and I started our journey that what happens to your husband happens to you. In case you haven't noticed (you probably have), I didn't know that truth when Abraham and I left Haran. Abraham and I were one in God's eyes, but it took 24 years and a personal visitation from God and two angels[59] before I could conceive that when He spoke to Abraham, He was speaking to me.

I was learning in my faith, day by day, just as you are. Sometimes, if we're not careful, we make the mistake of thinking we're born into God's family fully mature. That mistake leads to self-disqualification as we think we should know more than we do or that we can do more than we can. God wants us to mature at His side. He leads us to and through experiences that allow that to happen. In His kindness, He calls us His "children" as a reminder that there is always growing up to do, even for 90-year-old matriarchs and their 100-year-old husbands.

In the first few days and weeks after the Visitors left, I struggled with the reality of what that whole encounter meant. I was going to have a baby. I wasn't going to find one or adopt one or make something work. I was going to have a baby.

Sure enough, like the young women I'd watched from a longing distance, the rounded belly of a promise kept began to grow. I felt this baby move and I giggled. I wondered which one of us he'd look more like and I laughed. I lost my balance, my feet swelled and I chuckled.

How could this be *happening*? How could this be happening *now*? How could this be happening now *for me*?

I just kept laughing. This was hard on my body as you can probably imagine, but the delight was greater. As El Shaddai promised, within a year I was gazing into the face of our newborn son. The moment of his birth was so extraordinarily joyful that we named him Isaac, which means (drum roll) "laughter."[60] Our laughter was a blessing, and Abraham and I could think of no better name for our son than the delight we both felt at the fulfillment of God's Promise.

As I suckled my tiny newborn miracle son close to my heart, he looked back at me with cypress-colored eyes, and my heart laughed again. My Isaac! My Laughter! My Delight!

PART OF THE PLAN
In Haran, El Shaddai spoke to Abram, "Go!" and then inhaled. Twenty-four years later, He exhaled, changed our names, and miraculously gave us a child. In my mind, I'd waited oh so long for The Promise, but to El Shaddai (Who created time and rules it) it was no more than the space between inhaling and exhaling. God breathes on you, and in the space of one breath, you go from Contentious Control Freak to Royal Princess, from Childless to Mother of Nations.

Waiting had always been part of El Shaddai's plan. The 24-year span between His inhale and His exhale was the time it took for Him to transform me into a princess whose heart was ready to believe Him. The Promise couldn't be entrusted to Sarai, whose contentious spirit created unease and instability that would have been passed on to her child. The Promise had to come from royalty, from Sarah clothed in gentleness, quietness, strength, and dignity.

Delay wasn't unique to the realization of El Shaddai's Promise to Abraham and me. It's part of His plan for fulfillment in all of His children of Promise. There are seasons when the road He's set you upon seems endless, but God does not hold His breath. When you find yourself waiting for God to exhale, cling to Him (*qavah*), then dig in and prepare for what's next (*chaqah*) as He draws out the royalty within.

Having come so far in distance, age, and transformation, you might think my journey was now complete; that because the fulfillment of God's Promise lay swaddled in my arms His work in and through me was finished. Not so. There was still one more task to accomplish as my part of the perpetuation of God's plan. It was perhaps the most difficult of all. Now, I had to put my house in order.

MAKING PEACE

As was customary, Abraham threw a great feast when I weaned Isaac. Four thousand-plus years ago, more than half of children didn't survive until their third birthdays. Malnutrition and disease were rampant child killers, as were wild animals, parasites, snakes, scorpions, and, yes, spiders. Reaching this milestone was cause for celebration because it meant he'd survived his most uncertain years.

Abraham and I *tsachaq*-ed, (we laughed), in delight that day as we watched our friends and family celebrating the life of our Laughter, our *itzak*,[61] our Isaac. There was food and music and dancing. Like most three-year-olds, Isaac was eager to explore and assert his independence so I let him roam about the tables on his own—a bit. Of course, he was always only a few steps away. As I watched, Ishmael, who now was 17, approached Isaac. Unaware that I was listening, he began to mock and tease my child.[62]

Ishmael had always been competitive and as aggressive as a wild donkey,[63] but watching him with Isaac I discerned more than brotherly competition. It was contention and rivalry. I knew firsthand the destructive power of contention; it was all too familiar to me. I knew what it sounded like, what it felt like, and I knew what I saw and heard was not just brotherly jesting; it was hateful contention. Just beyond the teasing and rivalry was the frightening ferocity of jealousy.

Ishmael fell silent as I approached and took Isaac into my arms. Our eyes met. He knew I'd seen him, that I'd heard his antagonistic jabs. He walked away without a word. He knew I knew.

My Greatest Grandson would describe what I saw that day: "Out of the abundance of the heart, the mouth speaks."[64] I knew what was in Ishmael's heart because I heard it. This wasn't an attitude; this was a belief, a belief based on a false sense of entitlement. Where two differing beliefs occupy the same house, there can be no peace.

I weighed what I saw and heard and felt, and the heaviness of it threatened to crush my heart. I wanted to be wrong. I wanted Ishmael to love Isaac. I wanted peace to just "happen." All my wanting would never make it so. I knew what I had to do—I could not make nice, I had to make peace. The only solution stole my breath away. One of them had to leave. There was no question who would stay.

HARD TO HEAR
I wasn't sure I'd have the strength to do what had to be

done, so I practiced the faith that had grown in me and talked to El Shaddai. Then, confident in my discernment, I waited for the right moment to tell Abraham. After our evening meal a few days later, in the cool of the evening, that moment came.

"Sarah, you've been preoccupied the last few days. What's on your mind?"

As I was learning that He would, El Shaddai prepared a way. The step I was about to take would be painful—not just for me. But I knew it was the right way, just as I knew El Shaddai would be with me—and with Abraham, who I would be taking with me down this cheerless-for-a-time road.

"I never can hide my mind from you for very long." I looked at him as directly yet tenderly as possible. After more than a half a century of marriage, Abraham and I often knew each other's thoughts without a spoken word. I wondered if he already knew what I was going to say.

As I looked into his eyes, knowing that soon I would see pain in them, I found the courage to step onto the road before us: "I'm concerned about what I see happening with Ishmael and Isaac."

Instantly, the pain I knew was coming showed in his kind eyes. His next words were cautious, as though he knew this conversation was the beginning of another painful part of our journey.

"What do you see, Sarah?"

I could not make this pretty. I could not make this better. I could only speak the truth quickly and succinctly: "Ishmael mocks Isaac."

"Oh, Sarah, is it not that Ishmael is enjoying his little brother? Brothers are like that."

"No, Abraham." He heard my tone. I heard my tone. This was not as I'd spoken in the past. This was a necessary truth. "Ishmael does not enjoy his brother. Ishmael mocks his brother. His words are full of jealousy and mockery, bitterness and... danger."

"Are you sure, Sarah? Is there any way you could have misunderstood Ishmael's words or intent?"

The pain was now in his voice, which almost trembled as he questioned me. How I wanted to be wrong! I wasn't.

"Oh, Abraham, if only I could say I was mistaken! But I know what I saw and heard. For Isaac's sake, you have to send Hagar and Ishmael away. Your two sons can never share an inheritance."[65]

Ishmael was no less Abraham's son than Isaac, and he loved both sons equally. Ishmael had been Abraham's shadow for years. At 17, Ishmael was entering manhood and the father-son relationship was taking on a deeper intimacy. Sending Ishmael away was too great a sorrow for Abraham to face alone. Grieving, he went to God for help. [66]

When he reached a quiet place, both in his heart and for his body, God spoke: "Don't feel badly about the boy and your maid. Do whatever Sarah tells you. Your descendants will come through Isaac. Regarding your maid's son, be assured that I'll also develop a great nation from him—he's your son, too." [67]

God's answer was hard to hear, but as always, Abraham was faithful to do as God said. The next morning Abraham gave Hagar and Ishmael some water and some food and sent them away. [68]

God's answers to your prayers are always just. That doesn't mean the answer is what you hope to hear. Abraham wasn't the only one who wept as Ishmael turned from us and walked into the wilderness. I loved Ishmael. He was my stepson, raised in my home. I held him as a baby, taught him as a child, comforted him, fed him, laughed with him, cried with him. Still, despite how difficult losing Ishmael was, I knew the Covenant and its fulfillment had begun in us, Abraham and me, through

Isaac, and the condition of our household would either help or hinder that fulfillment. The Promise El Shaddai had begun had to be nurtured in order to thrive and the contention and strife that were swirling overhead could not be allowed to continue.

IT WAS ME—AGAIN

For me, the pain of losing Ishmael was worsened because I knew with more certainty than anyone the cause of this pain. It was me. Again. Ishmael was the handiwork of my unbelief, conceived in one moment when I grew tired of waiting on The Promise, turned my back on the Promise Maker, and played God in my life; one moment of self-will that resulted in an eternity of consequences greater than my mind could fathom. Through my unbelief, I'd inserted an imitation heir whose continued presence in our home could be a threat to God's chosen Promise Bearer. Ishmael and the pain we all now would have to endure were a direct result of my unbelief.

There was no condemnation of Hagar or Ishmael in our decision to send them away, and this wasn't another of my schemes to control an outcome. I was neither manipulating Abraham to ensure Isaac received his inheritance, nor was I being vindictive toward Hagar. The decision to send them away was simply a declaration: "This is the son God promised. This is what God told us to do. That isn't."

We're all capable of creating counterfeits in our lives, something that looks almost exactly like what God promised, but isn't because it was created in a moment when you decided you'd waited long enough. It seemed to you that God apparently wasn't going to answer your prayer, and you'd have to take matters in your own hands to ensure a desirable outcome.

Take a moment to look at your life. If you are struggling somewhere, it may be because you've created a counterfeit. I must caution you not to act rashly. Not all struggles are the result of a counterfeit in your life and the road upon which you embark can lead to darker, more painful places if you begin the journey without wise counsel. First, seek wisdom from El Shaddai, and if necessary, seek the counsel of a trusted mentor. If it becomes clear that, "This is the thing God said, and this is the thing God didn't say that I made up and allowed to come into my life," ask God next for the faith and courage to become a peacemaker.

BLESSED PEACEMAKERS

A Counterfeit cohabitating with a Covenant creates the potential for a Compromise. A Compromise runs parallel to a Promise. It looks like the Promise, could be made to fit into the Promise, but it isn't the Promise so it lacks power and purpose. It is tempting to alleviate the Conflict that arises between the Counterfeit and the Covenant by introducing the Compromise. However, because it lacks power and purpose, any solution the

Compromise provides to the Conflict will be temporary. To end the Conflict, you must make peace

Speaking a few thousand years after Abraham and I completed our journey, Jesus said, "Blessed are the peacemakers, for they will be called the children of God" (Matthew 5:9). He didn't say, "Blessed are the peace**keepers**" because there's a world of difference between keeping peace and making peace.

Keeping peace is compromising to avoid confrontation. It's sweeping broken glass under a rug, wincing silently when a splinter works its way through the fibers, then bending over to sweep it back—until next time. Keeping peace is conciliation to avoid dealing with life's difficult issues. It's appeasement to perpetuate a fantasy that "Everything's fine. Everybody's happy." Keeping peace is living in fear.

Making peace is facing heart-level issues with confidence born from authenticity. It's confronting conflict-creating counterfeits then fearlessly yet lovingly proclaiming Truth into the situation. It's living according to the call of God's Spirit. [69] Making peace is living by faith.

Peace doesn't just happen. Creating an environment of peace takes action. Psalm 34:14 says to "seek peace and pursue it." The word "seek" is the Hebrew word transliterated *baqash,* and means to "demand," "require," even "plead" for.[70] "Pursue" is the Hebrew *radaph,* which means (among other things) to "chase" or "hunt".[71] Demand and hunt aren't words of timidity. It takes boldness to *baqash* and *radaph*.

Peacemakers hunt peace down and compel it to be made. That doesn't mean you demand in a contentious way as a child throwing a tantrum. It means you don't settle for less than complete resolution and peace in the situation.

> Peacekeeping is circumstantial and conditional. Peacemaking is built on truth, regardless of circumstances or conditions.

> Peacekeeping is fairly easy—you just ignore, or pretend or "live and let live". Peacemaking calls for action and courage—a great deal of courage.

FAITH AND COURAGE

For Abraham and me making peace meant having the faith and courage to say good-bye to a son we both loved. We mourned as we watched Ishmael's silhouette fade into the horizon, but our sorrow was lightened because we knew God was Enough to protect Ishmael and provide a way for him even in the desert—just as He'd done for us. We didn't need to know what Ishmael would find in the wilderness he walked into because the One Who created the wilderness had promised to provide and protect. We had faith in our faithful Promise Maker.

The thought of confronting a counterfeit in life is daunting. Believe me, I know. Telling Abraham that Ishmael had to leave for Isaac's sake was the most difficult conversation I ever had with my husband, even more difficult than offering him my handmaid as a second wife. However, if you're certain you've created a counterfeit somewhere in your life, your choices are to keep peace and live in fear or to make peace and live by faith. God will provide the faith and courage you need. Just ask Him and then move forward in obedience. You can't see what's beyond that dark curve in the road, but you know Who made the road. He is walking it with you.

As promised, God blessed Ishmael and made him the father of the Ishmaelite nation mentioned throughout your Old Testament. I wasn't there to witness the peace that developed and persisted between Isaac and Ishmael over time, but your Bible says that when "Abraham breathed his last and died at a good old age, an old man and full of years…His sons Isaac and Ishmael buried him." [72]

Upon Abraham's death, Isaac reached out to his older half-brother to join him in honoring and mourning their father. And Ishmael came. There was harmony between Abraham's two sons because decades earlier their father and I had the faith and courage to make peace.

OUR FAITHFUL PROMISE MAKER

When Isaac was a child, before he was old enough to spend days out with his father, he'd often "help" me with tasks around our encampment. He particularly delighted in helping bake his father's favorite barley bread. His help usually consisted of fetching me a bowl or passing me a bottle of oil.

After I mixed the dough together, I'd give him a small lump, which he'd gleefully roll, pound, and mash into shapes while I patted out the bread to bake for our meal. When Abraham came home in the evening, Isaac would fidget with excitement waiting for his father to taste the bread "we" had baked. Abraham and I would exchange knowing smiles as we praised Isaac's baking skills.

The covenant God made with Abraham that dark night in the desert is chiseled into the bedrock of Eternity as the foundation for the relationship between God and man, and yet man's involvement in that timeless Promise amounted to Isaac helping me bake bread. That Abraham gathered the animals had nothing to do with the contract. That he cut them in half and chased away the vultures had nothing to do with the contract. Abraham's participation was as peripheral as Isaac's fetching me a mixing bowl.

God the Creator of the universe neither needed nor asked anything of significance from Abraham in making the covenant. He didn't ask Abraham to give his word or swear an oath. He didn't require him to walk through the blood path. In fact, God asked nothing of him except his company. Abraham was present simply because God enjoyed the relationship He and Abraham shared.

The passing through the blood that made and sealed the covenant was all God. Mankind has been on the blessings side of that moonless-night covenant for more than four millennia and will continue to reap those blessings through all time, even though mankind's delegate slept through the entire process. The forging of God's covenant with man, was and is eternally all God's doing.

THE GARDEN-GATE PROMISE

On the Day of Laughter, Sovereign God sat outside my tent, ate hot barley bread and spoke life to my dead faith to resurrect my dead womb. El Shaddai left heaven to pay a personal visit to a 90-year-old woman who'd spent all her life either worshiping false gods or playing god so that I could believe, receive, and conceive. As wonderful and miraculous as His blessings to me that day were, the real reason for His visit was not to give me a son but to give you a Savior.

The Promise that fueled our journey to the Promised Land was the perpetuation of a Promise that preceded Abraham and me by more than two thousand years. The covenant God made with Abraham that dark night in the desert established the descendants of Abraham and me as the vehicle through which God would fulfill The Promise He made to my greatest grandmother, Eve.

My son, Isaac, was Eve's eighteen-greats grandson through her son Seth, who was the six-greats grandfather of Noah. Yes, Noah of the Ark and The Flood and the People-Saving God we'd heard whispers about back in Sumer. Abraham and I didn't know we were direct descendants of that remnant of humanity God saved. We also didn't know one of our Direct Descendants someday would be the Salvation of all humanity.

Just before Eve left The Garden, God vowed that One of her issue would one day crush the head of the serpent whose lies for a time stole paradise from mankind:

> *"And I will put enmity between you and the woman, and between your offspring and hers; He will crush your head, and you will strike His heel"* (Genesis 3:15 NIV).

Isaac's birth was pivotal in the Story of Eternity not because it was the fulfillment of The Promise to Abraham and me. Isaac was the first born of the nation of Israel, the people God chose as the means through which His

Garden-Gate Promise of Redemption would be fulfilled in all creation. I told you previously that my laughter was the beginning of my righteousness; it was also the beginning of yours because it was the trumpet sound ushering in the coming of Jesus, the Savior Messiah through Whom you have been declared righteous and Whose lineage traces back directly to my Laughter.

THERE IS A WAY

I don't know where you are in your journey, whether you're just starting out or have worn through several pairs of sandals. I don't know if you're skipping through green garden pathways or trudging through ankle-deep sand in a wilderness. Regardless, I know you need a Guide. We all do.

El Shaddai provides a Guide. It's His Spirit living in you. Just as He breathed on me and made His Spirit part of who I am, when you choose to walk the path He's designed, His Spirit becomes part of who you are. The Spirit provides all the faith, courage, and wisdom you need for the journey.

You're never too old and it's never too late to step onto the path He's prepared for you. You've never wandered so far off that one step in a different direction won't set your feet on the road toward God's Promise. No matter how many sandstorms have blown through or how deeply buried beneath a sand dune, no heart is ever lost to God. There is a Way.

The Way was made more than two thousand years ago when the very hands on which your name is engraved were nailed to a cross. Jesus, the Son of God, El Shaddai in human form, provided His life as the sacrifice that was Enough to atone for every misstep and every stumble. His resurrection opened the gate to give you access to eternal life, should you so choose.

IT'S ALL GOD

At the beginning of our journey, I told you Abraham and I left Haran chasing a Promise. Standing at the end of the road looking back to where we started, my perspective is so different. It almost makes me laugh when I think about it now, how Abraham and I thought we had so much to *do* to ensure The Promise was fulfilled.

God makes Promises and then *He* fulfills them. No matter how far off the path you wander, how lost your heart or dead your faith, how many times you've played God then blamed Him for the counterfeits you've created, the joy of my heart to share with you is you can never be so foolish that you can undo the Promise of God. He brings His Promises to completion because "the gifts and the calling of God are irrevocable."[73] And He does it regardless of all our schemes and detours. "Faithful is He who called you, and He will bring it to pass" (1 Thessalonians 5:24 NASB). *He* brings it to pass, not you. You can't make it happen, you can't give it back, and you can't undo it.

Abraham did nothing to establish God's desert covenant except show up and believe. His part in forging that mysterious, eternal bond between humanity and Deity culminated in Abraham resting while God did all the "work." God, Whose ways never waver, expects no more from you. There's nothing for you to do to reap the blessings of God's Promise except believe.

You don't have to perform. You don't have to serve. You don't have to prove yourself worthy of The Promise through sacrifice or busy-ness. You can't earn what He's already given you.

God does it all. He always does.

YOU CAN CHOOSE

My need to control an outcome led Abraham and me into dangerous and nearly tragic territory, but The Promise was always secure because it was never in my hands. None of my meddling and manipulating could make The Promise manifest prior to God's ordained time. None of my missteps or mistakes could stop the fulfillment of The Promise because it was never under my control. Every time I detoured, it was His hand that led me back, that delivered me and saved me from myself.

I'm not a special case. He does the same for everyone who chooses to believe Him. He has done it for you, even if you haven't yet conceived it. If your journey to this point has been a solo excursion, it doesn't have to be for one more step. If the road you're on seems to be nothing but sandstorms and dead ends, there's a Way to change direction. If fear has ruled your life, holding you hostage behind a facade of imposed identity, you can drop the veil.

You can choose a different path; you don't have to be who you've always been. You can discard your robes of fear and dress your heart in gentleness and peace, knowing even when the path of your life ends, The Promise carries you beyond what your eyes see into the unseen Eternal. That's The Promise God gives you, the way Jesus made for you. All you need is to receive it from Him.

The kindness of God leads us to Him, no matter how obscure the path, how wide the wilderness, or how willful our heading. God heaps kindness into our lives in giant spoonfuls and bids us feast. It's an all-you-can eat buffet: No lines, no limits, and no end to the supply. His kindness removes all condemnation, leads us to repentance, and ultimately to healing.

God didn't leave me to suffer in the desert a quarrelsome, barren old woman with no hope, no heart, no faith, and no future. Instead, He lavished me with kindness, called me His Princess, and then filled my heart with laughter.

LAUGH WITH ME
I'm not sure what I expected to happen when Abraham and I set off toward the edge of the world west of Haran

when I was a young woman of 65, but I know there were some things I certainly did not expect: I didn't expect that I would never see my homeland again. I didn't expect to spend time in Pharaoh's harem in Egypt. I didn't expect to give my husband to another woman. I didn't expect to become a stepmother. I certainly never expected God would know—and then change—my name. I didn't expect to laugh a laugh that would echo through Eternity or that at 90 I would birth Laughter. But as I said when you and I started this trip, life seldom turns out as we expect.

It's life's uncertainty that makes the need for a Guide so pressing. Left to navigate for ourselves, we can manipulate our lives into disaster. I almost did—more than once. Facing the unknown as you do every day, the temptation to forge your own path, to take a shortcut, or even choose to stop moving altogether at times can be overwhelming. Fear of the unknown stops us in our tracks as often as it makes us run.

You can face the future not with fear but with laughter. The way to do that is found in the *Book of Proverbs* in your Bible, and believe it or not, it's all about how you're dressed. It took me nearly 100 years to learn this Future Facing Fashion Tip. Here it is:

> *"She is clothed with strength and dignity and she laughs without fear of the future" (Proverb 31:25 NLT).*

Strength and dignity are the perfect accessories for facing an unknown, but you can't buy them at any bazaar, even in your time. They are byproducts of a gentle and quiet spirit, again not available in any store, not even with all your "online" (whatever that is) shopping. There's only one place to find such finery with which to adorn your inner self. They are gifts from El Shaddai when you believe.

Like the Apostle Paul, I, too, have a prayer for you. I pray that you would be delighted in what you believe; that you would believe that nothing is too difficult for God; believe that it's never too late to start over; believe that your heart is never beyond the call of His kindness; and believe that it's never too late for God to fulfill His promises. I pray you believe and your faith funnel opens wide so God can pour His grace into your life. I pray His grace brings new life that floods your heart so that it overflows in joyous laughter.

Your Bible records my hope for you from the moment I saw the face of my precious Isaac. I knew it was God Who had made me laugh with Him in delight at such a reason-defying fulfillment of such a glorious Promise. God made me laugh then gave me Laughter. My prayer that day and this is that you will not only understand the source of my laughter, but you will hear my laughter—really hear it, deeply and purely.

> *"And Sarah said, 'God has made me laugh. All*

who hear will laugh with me'" (Genesis 21:6 NLV).

All who hear will laugh with me.

Shalom.

ENDNOTES

[1] Provine, Robert, *A Big Mystery: Why do we laugh?*, retrieved at http://www.nbcnews.com/id/3077386/ns/technology_and_science-science/t/big-mystery-why-do-we-laugh/#.WcLO5MiGOUl (April 2017).

[2] Genesis 18:10 (The Message Bible).

[3] *"Know therefore that the Lord your God is God; He is the faithful God, keeping His covenant of love to a thousand generations of those who love Him and keep his commandments"* Deuteronomy 7:9 (NASB).

[4] *Dissecting Mesopotamian Jewelry*, retrieved at https://allmesopotamia.wordpress.com/2012/07/24/dissecting-mesopotamian-jewelry (May 2017).

[5] *Sumerian Clothing and Dress*, retrieved at http://history-world.org/sumeria,%20dress.htm (March 2017).

[6] *Ancient Mesopotamian Religion,* retrieved at https://en.wikipedia.org/wiki/Ancient_Mesopotamian_religion#Deities (March 2017).

[7] Retrieved at http://islam101.net/index.php/history/11-prophet-ibrahim/3-2100-bc-the-city-of-ur (May 2017).

[8] *"Sarai was barren; she had no child"* Genesis 11:30 (NASB).

[9] Nanna (or Sin) was the name of the Sumerian moon god. He was the city god of both Haran and Ur of the Chaldeans, and the god of fertility.

[10] Genesis 12:1–3.

[11] Retrieved at http://www.ancient-origins.net/human-origins-religions/sumerian-seven-top-ranking-gods-sumerian-pantheon-007787 (March 2017).

[12] Retrieved at http://www.answers.com/Q/How_fast_did_ancient_caravans_travel#slide=60 (March 2017).

[13] *"Abram passed through the land as far as the site of Shechem, to the oak of Moreh. Now the Canaanite was then in the land. The Lord appeared to Abram and said, 'To your descendants I will give this land.' So he built an altar there to the Lord who had appeared to him"* Genesis 12:6–7(NASB).

[14] Retrieved at http://bibleatlas.org/great_sea.htm (May 2017).

[15] *Tents*, retrieved at http://www.dabhand.org/

MannersAndCustoms/tents.htm (May 2017).

[16] *Amorites*, retrieved at https://en.wikipedia.org/wiki/Amorites (May 2017).

[17] Retrieved at https://en.wikipedia.org/wiki/Canaan (May 2017).

[18] *Innana*, retrieved at https://en.wikipedia.org/wiki/Inanna (May 2017).

[19] Ibid.

[20] Kadari, Tamar, *Sarah: Midrash and Aggadah*, retrieved at https://jwa.org/encyclopedia/article/sarah-midrash-and-aggadah (Dec. 2017).

[21] Ibid.

[22] Ibid.

[23] Retrieved at http://biblehub.com/hebrew/6960a.htm.

[24] Retrieved at http://biblehub.com/hebrew/2442.htm.

[25] Genesis 12:18-19 (NIV).

[26] Genesis 13:1-11 (NIV).

[27] Genesis 14:13 (NIV).

[28] Genesis 15:7 (NIV).

[29] *Steps of Ancient Covenant Making*, retrieved at http://www.thectp.org/Notes/Inheritance/Inheritance_2.pdf (May 2017).

[30] Genesis 15:4 (NASB)

[31] Genesis 16:4 (NIV).

[32] Genesis 16:5–6 (paraphrased).

[33] Retrieved at http://biblehub.com/greek/1457b.htm (Aug. 2017).

[34] *"I am the Lord; that is my name! I will not yield my glory to another or my praise to idols"* Isaiah 42:8 (NIV).

[35] Genesis 16:13.

[36] Genesis 16:7–9 (NASB).

[37] Genesis 16:11 (paraphrased NASB).

[38] Genesis 17:15–16.

[39] Genesis 17:5.

[40] Retrieved at http://www.hebrew4christians.com/

Grammar/Unit_One/Aleph-Bet/Hey/hey.html (Dec. 2017).

[41] *Hope of Israel Ministries, Secret Code of the Hebrew Alphabet The Awesome Mystery of the Hebrew "Hay"[h] and "Vav"[v],* retrieved at http://www.hope-of-israel.org/hay&vav.htm (Dec. 2017).

[42] Ezekiel 36:26 (NIV).

[43] Ephesians 4:24 (ESV).

[44] Genesis 1:2, *ruach*, retrieved at http://biblehub.com/genesis/1-2.htm, http://biblehub.com/hebrew/7307.htm (Aug. 2017).

[45] Genesis 18:1–3 (NIV).

[46] Genesis 18:9 (NIV).

[47] Ibid.

[48] Ibid.

[49] Genesis 18:12 (NIV, paraphrased).

[50] Genesis 18:12 (NIV).

[51] Genesis 18:13–14 (NIV).

[52] Genesis 18:15 (NIV).

[53] Retrieved at http://biblehub.com/hebrew/6711.htm (Sept. 2017).

[54] Genesis 3:8 (NIV).

[55] Romans 2:4 (Berean Study Bible).

[56] *The Voice Bible.*

[57] Romans 10:10 (NASB).

[58] Genesis 15:5–6 (paraphrased).

[59] *The Identity of the Three Visitors in Genesis 18*, retrieved at https://www.bible-bridge.com/the-identity-of-the-three-visitors-in-genesis-18 (Jan. 2018).

[60] *Itzak*, retrieved at http://biblehub.com/hebrew/3327.htm (Jan. 2018).

[61] Ibid.

[62] Genesis 21:8–9 (NIV).

[63] Genesis 16:12 (NIV).

[64] Matthew 12:34 (NKJV).

[65] Genesis 21:8-11 (NIV).

[66] Genesis 21:11 (NIV).

[67] Genesis 21:12–13 (The Message Bible).

[68] Genesis 21:14 (NIV).

[69] *And let the peace that comes from Christ rule in your hearts. For as members of one body you are called to live in peace. And always be thankful"* Colossians 3:15 (NLT).

[70] Retrieved at http://biblehub.com/hebrew/1245.htm (Sept. 2017).

[71] Retrieved at http://biblehub.com/hebrew/7291.htm (Sept. 2017).

[72] Genesis 25:8–9 (NIV).

[73] Romans 11:29 (NASB).

CONNECT WITH PAIGE

Paige has been a Bible teacher and speaker for well over 20 years. Although the Genesis Girls series has been a favorite over the years, Paige's favorite thing is simply the Bible. The Word and words of God are the fuel of her life. She doesn't come to bring "Her Thing," her desire is to come alongside whomever shepherds the people—to surround and protect, give aid and relief to that body of believers and their leadership. She brings clear understanding and revelation of Scripture through well-studied messages delivered with humor and real, clear application.

Contact her for retreats, conferences or special events.
paige.henderson@fellowshipofthesword.com

FURTHER CONNECTION

Paige and her husband Richard co-founded Fellowship of the Sword Ministries in 2003. Through week-long retreat-styled encounters, men and women can be reset, restored, and encouraged in very real and relevant ways in relationship to a very real and relevant God.

About Fellowship of the Sword

The Vision is to see people live life free.

The Mission is to serve the Church by facilitating catalytic encounters with God for the purpose of uncovering truth, unlocking identity and unleashing passion.

Now without faith it is impossible to please God, for the one who draws near to Him [the catalytic encounter], *must believe that He exists and rewards those who seek Him* [the 2 bedrock principles of discipleship]. Hebrews 11:6

The mission is achieved through an event called Quest, and it is available for men and women. These events occur—one for men and one for women—every month. As of this publication, the ministry has venues in Texas, Missouri, Georgia, England and Bulgaria. To discover more about the ministry (Please do!) or to register for an event (A great idea!) go to fellowshipofthesword.com. An excellent and gifted Somebody will get in touch with you to answer any questions you may have or assist you in the registration process.

Printed in Great Britain
by Amazon